the Pontifical North American College

Celebrating 150 Years of Priestly Formation in the Eternal City

the Pontifical North American College

CELEBRATING 150 YEARS OF PRIESTLY FORMATION IN THE ETERNAL CITY

Making Everlasting Memories, L.L.C. Cincinnati, Ohio

This book is dedicated to

POPE BENEDICT XVI

The Pontifical North American College: Celebrating 150 Years of Priestly Formation in the Eternal City © 2010 *Making Everlasting Memories*®. All rights reserved. No part of this book may be reproduced in any form or by any electronic or mechanical means including information storage and retrieval systems without permission in writing from the publishers or the Pontifical North American College. Published by MeM-*Making Everlasting Memories, L.L.C.*, 11475 Northlake Drive, Cincinnati, OH 45249. (888) 549-4636, www.MeM.com. First edition.

11 10 09 08 07   5 4 3 2 1

Library of Congress Cataloging-in-Publication Data

ISBN-13   978-0-9798851-1-2
ISBN-10   0-9798851-1-6

SAN 854-6592

Designed by: *Making Everlasting Memories, L.L.C.*
Production coordinated by: *Making Everlasting Memories, L.L.C.*
Printed and bound by: *PrintManagement, L.L.C.*

PAGE 2: Men of the North American College prostrate themselves as the *Litany of the Saints* is chanted during the diaconate ordination in St. Peter's Basilica.

PAGE 4: Pope Benedict XVI during his Sunday Angelus address with the New Men of the College.

RIGHT: Seminarians process into the Chapel of the Immaculate Conception for Mass.

PAGE 8: The Most Reverend John J. Myers, Archbishop of Newark and Chairman of the Board of Governors.

PAGE 10: Msgr. James F. Checchio, the College's 22nd Rector, greets Pope Benedict XVI at the Vatican in 2006.

PAGE 12: Seminarians Gregory Ihm (Diocese of Madison) and Anthony Lickteig (Archdiocese of Washington) at prayer.

Table of Contents

"Truly, the North American College is America's Seminary in Rome."

Letter from the Chairman of the Board

My Dear Friends in Christ,

It is my honor to serve as Chairman of the Board of Governors of the Pontifical North American College during this year of its Sesquicentennial Anniversary.

When the College was founded 150 years ago, it welcomed a first year class of thirteen seminarians representing eight dioceses from six states ranging from New York to California. With gratitude to God for the many blessings of the past century and one half, the College now serves more than two hundred twenty-five students in seminary formation, more than seventy priests in its graduate house, and numerous priests each year on sabbatical. Today, the College serves more than one hundred thirteen dioceses representing forty states, the District of Columbia and Australia! Truly, the North American College is *America's Seminary in Rome*.

The role of priestly leadership in the Church in our day necessitates a great responsibility to nurture faithfully and diligently and to develop vocations to the holy priesthood. Thanks to the dedicated effort of many people over many years, the College has excelled in fulfilling this responsibility.

The alumni of the College have helped shape and nurture the Catholic Church in America. They have led the faithful into closer union with Our Lord through the sacraments and by passing on the truths of the faith effectively. They have participated in the new evangelization by creatively developing ministries in their parishes and dioceses. They have been faithful leaders in the local and universal Church. Thus, the story of the Pontifical North American College is of interest not only to alumni and friends but to all people who care for the Catholic Church and pray for good, holy, and zealous priests.

As you read this story of the College, I hope that you will be edified and inspired by the tremendous dedication of the many people who have made this ministry possible. From architects to artists, from rectors to repetitors -- the College has been a place where people have used their talents for the greater good and have worked tirelessly to make steadfast in the Lord the many priestly hearts entrusted to them.

I hope that you will have a chance to visit the College in the near future to see for yourself how the reality of this story is lived out today in the seminary, the graduate house of studies, and the priests' sabbatical program.

Ad Multos Annos!

Sincerely in the Lord,

Most Rev. John J. Myers, JCD, DD, Archbishop of Newark
Chairman of the Board of Governors of the Pontifical North American College

"...strengthen their faith and their love for the Roman Pontiff."

Letter from the Rector

Praised be Jesus Christ!

According to a joyful report by a correspondent in Rome, after the official Mass and Papal audience with Blessed Pius IX marking the opening of the College on December 8, 1859, there were high hopes expressed for the Pontifical North American College! He wrote of the festivities of that day, "Thus the Americans have taken possession of their, from henceforth, *'Alma Mater'*, and if the fruits correspond to a beginning so full of hope, America will yet, in years to come, treasure the precious memory of the eighth of December, 1859."

Indeed, we still honor this beautiful Solemnity of the Immaculate Conception of Mary and I would say that there is as much hope now as there was back in 1859. Since its opening, over 5,000 young men have come to this College for seminary formation, over 1,000 priests have come for graduate studies and many more have come to Rome to enjoy spiritual and theological renewal in our Institute for Continuing Theological Education. Grounded in Jesus Christ through liturgical and private prayer, well trained in the teachings of our faith, and full of filial devotion to Christ's Vicar, these men have all shared a common mission - sent forth to preach the Gospel, to care for the spiritual needs of the faithful, and to be immersed in the work of evangelization.

It is my honor and privilege to serve as Rector of the College and participate in this good and hopeful ministry each day. It is my wish that through this book, you will come to know more about the College and those who have been a part of its life over the past 150 years and that you will join in our mission as well. I ask you to pray for the many young men who are currently in formation to be priests and for those priests engaged in ongoing formation here in Rome. Pray too that we will continue to be faithful to our mission, so simply but succinctly written in Latin above the principal entrance to the College, that *the young men who have come here from the distant shores of America, looking upon the Vatican Hill, strengthen their faith and their love for the Roman Pontiff.*

Vergine Immaculata, Aiutateci!

Sincerely yours in Christ,

Rev. Msgr. James F. Checchio, JCD, MBA
Rector of the Pontifical North American College

150th Anniversary Prayer

Almighty God and Father,
Master and Lord of the harvest,
we come before you
grateful for the generous and noble souls
of all those who have been associated
with the Pontifical North American College
since its founding by Blessed Pope Pius IX:
our seminarians and alumni,
faculty and staff,
rectors and bishops,
friends and benefactors.

We look upon the Virgin Mother of Your Son,
under the title of her Immaculate Conception as our patroness
and trust in her intercession.

Like her, may we always be obedient to your will,
assiduous in meditating on your Word,
ponder the mysteries of the faith through study and prayer,
and love those entrusted to our care.

Send an abundance of laborers into your harvest;
reward with eternal life all those who for your sake do good to us;
and when our earthly journeys will have come to an end
may we all hear from the most just Judge of all,
"Well done, good and faithful servant,
enter into the joy of your Lord."

We ask this through Christ our Lord.

Amen

The Pontifical North American College

For 150 years, men have journeyed to the Pontifical North American College to nurture their priestly vocations. There in the heart of the Church, they live close to the ministry of the Holy Father, deepen their theological education and experience the rich universality of Catholicism.

Founded in 1859 by Pope Pius IX as a house of priestly formation, the College has grown in its service to the

> "To this place looking towards the Vatican Hill young men come from the distant shores of America to strengthen their Faith and their Love of the Roman Pontiff."
>
> -- Inscription carved over the principal entrance of the College

American Church with opportunities for clergy to pursue both graduate studies and sabbatical renewal. More than 5,000 men have attended the College, returning to their home dioceses with an enriched vision of themselves, their Church and their world. The College also enhances the religious experience for American visitors to the Eternal City. The Bishop's Office for United States Visitors to the Vatican moves guests from tourist to pilgrim with opportunities to witness the history of the Catholic faith and hear the Holy Father communicate the teachings of the Church.

In this Year for Priests, the North American College celebrates its Sesquicentennial Anniversary as the bridge between the United States and the ancient See of St. Peter. We ask Our Lady of Humility to gain for our College and its alumni all the necessary graces to continue serving faithfully her Divine Son, Jesus Christ, Our Lord.

Ad multos annos!

Page 14: A view of St. Peter's Basilica from the roof of the North American College.

Page 15: Portrait of Our Lady of Humility which hangs behind the high altar in the Casa Santa Maria Chapel.

Page 16: Seminarian James Yamauchi (Diocese of Dallas) takes part in the College's annual Thanksgiving Day feast.

Above Left: His Eminence John Cardinal Foley celebrates Mass on the College's Patronal Feast of the Immaculate Conception.

Above Right: Kevin Regan (Archdiocese of Washington) in the main sacristy wearing the College's traditional house-cassock.

Right: Ryan Bredemeyer (Diocese of Peoria) on a mission trip to India. The College sponsors several excursions each year to give the men a new perspective on the spiritual and apostolic dimensions of the universal Church.

A Proposal by the Pontiff

It was the Roman Pontiff himself who proposed that a college be founded in Rome for the training of American diocesan clergy. In the early weeks of 1855, Pope Pius IX sent a letter to the bishops in America informing them of his intentions to found the seminary. The bishops initially responded with uncertainty about the funding and practicality of the project, but soon grew enthusiastic and, led by Archbishop Gaetano Bedini, took definite steps toward the realization of the Holy Father's idea.

Pius IX remained true to his promise to assist the American prelates in the establishment of the College and supplemented the funds they supplied. He also donated a locale for the new seminary conveniently situated in the historical center of the city, just a short walk from the Urban College of Propaganda where the men would attend classes. The building at 30 *Via dell' Umiltà* (Humility Street) dated to the 16th century and had served as a convent for both Dominican and Visitation nuns. It was perfectly fitting for seminary use with a *cortile*, a small Baroque chapel and space for 100 rooms.

A uniform was chosen for the seminarians with colors of both spiritual and patriotic significance—black cassocks with a red sash, white collar and blue trim. Archbishop Bedini himself completed another final detail, placing a portrait of Our Lady of Humility above the chapel's altar.

> "IF YOU ARE WILLING TO COMPLY WITH THIS DESIRE OF OURS—A DESIRE WHOSE SOLE PURPOSE IS THE SPIRITUAL BENEFIT OF YOUR TERRITORIES—WE WILL CERTAINLY NOT FAIL TO ASSIST YOU…SO THAT YOU CAN ESTABLISH THE COLLEGE."
>
> -- **POPE PIUS IX,** IN HIS LETTER TO THE AMERICAN BISHOPS

The American College was set to officially open on December 8, 1859.

America's Seminary in Rome

Festivities to inaugurate the American College commenced on December 7, 1859 with a procession from the *Piazza di Spagna* through the Roman streets to the door of the seminary's new home. Among those in the procession were the first 13 seminarians, representing six states and eight dioceses from coast to coast.

The College was formally dedicated the very next day on the feast of the Immaculate Conception under Her patronage. The day's events included a Pontifical High Mass celebrated by Archbishop Bedini, a special *pranzone* (festive mid-day meal) and a Papal audience at the Vatican with Pius IX.

> "...THE MOST HELPFUL SINGLE CONTRIBUTION WHICH THE HOLY SEE COULD MAKE TO THE WELFARE OF THE AMERICAN CLERGY..."
>
> -- FR. ROBERT MCNAMARA, '36

Finally established as a house of priestly formation, the College began to develop the routine and traditions which shaped it as an institution. The seminarians spent the majority of their day in rigorous study at the Urban College, and relied on frequent walks throughout the city for recreation, where they were broadened and influenced at the crossroads of civilization and Christendom.

The College marked another milestone in 1884, the celebratory year of its silver jubilee, when Pope Leo XIII decreed the canonical institution of the North American College and bestowed upon it the pontifical rank.

PAGE 18: Placard marking Humility Street, where the original College was opened in 1859.

PAGE 19: Pope Pius IX, founder of the North American College.

PAGE 20: The Casa Santa Maria stands in the heart of ancient Rome on the Via dell' Umiltà (Humility Street), number 30. The property has a long history, with foundations dating to 211 AD as a barracks for the municipal police and firemen of Rome under the Emperor Septimius Severus. More recently, it housed an order of Domincan nuns from 1598 to 1814, then a group of Visitation nuns from 1814 to 1858. It also served as a barracks for Napoleon's troops before being given to the Americans in 1859 as their first seminary in the Eternal City. Today, the original seminary serves as the graduate house of studies for American priests.

PAGE 21: This commemorative mosaic was done by the Vatican Mosaic Firm based on the sketches of Nello Ena, and is located outside the new seminary's main chapel. It portrays the original seminary on Humility Street and serves as a fitting reminder of the seminary's early years.

PAGE 22: The first men of the North American College. Seated are Anthony Zingsheim (Alton), Edward McGlynn (New York), Patrick Riordan (Chicago), Ambrose O'Neil (Albany), William Meriwether (Charleston). Standing are John Cassidy (San Francisco), Patrick Gibney (San Francisco), Claudian Northrop (Charleston), William Poole (Savannah), Ruben Parsons (New York), Michael Corrigan (Newark), Michael Clifford (Chicago), Robert Seton (New York).

ABOVE LEFT: Late 1600 bas-relief of the Assumption of the Blessed Virgin Mary done by Carlo Fontana, located above the entrance to the Casa Santa Maria Chapel.

ABOVE RIGHT: Mosaic depicting the Madonna and Child.

LEFT: Main doors of the Casa Santa Maria, flanked by the Coats of Arms of the College (above), the founder of the College, Pope Pius IX (right) and the present Pontiff, Benedict XVI (left).

LEFT: Present-day view of the refectory of the Casa Santa Maria. A portrait of Pius IX, the College's founder, hangs on the back wall. The portrait was given to the College by the Holy Father himself during his first visit to the College on January 29, 1860, the Feast of St. Francis de Sales. In his poignant address to the seminarians, he noted, "*arms and armies do not cause Us fear, but rather the perversion of ideas in which vice is taken for virtue and virtue for vice.*" The Holy Father beseeched the seminarians to be men of prayer, that powerful means through which human hearts could be healed and turned to God. Europe had found itself in a state of political and ideological upheaval since the 1700s, and in 1860, Italy raged with wars for unification. Pius IX himself was caught in the midst of the upheavals and was even forced into exile from 1848-1850. The Pope again visited the College in 1870, exactly ten years after his original visit. That year, with a heroic spirit, Pius' loyal sons at the American College offered these words to him as Rome was about to be taken by the unification movement, "*The following students of the American College of the United States offer themselves freely to Your Holiness so that you may make use of them in the army to protect the sacred rights of the Holy Roman Church during the siege.*" The students signed the letter, but the Pope was no longer the temporal ruler of Rome. During his reign, Pius IX officially declared the Dogma of the Immaculate Conception in 1854 and convened the First Vatican Council in 1868. Known for his personal devotion and holiness, Pius IX was beatified in 2000 by Pope John Paul II.

ABOVE: The men share a meal in the refectory to celebrate the seminary's 50th anniversary, 1909.

Right: Hallway leading to the Casa Santa Maria courtyard.

Below: The Red Room, located within the Casa Santa Maria, is an integral part of the College's rich history. During the Consistory ceremonies of the 1950s, American archbishops waited in the Red Room until the Pope had approved their names for elevation to the College of Cardinals. Today, the Red Room is used for faculty gatherings and the welcoming of ecclesiastical guests.

PAGE 26: One of the courtyards of the Casa Santa Maria serves as a place of prayer and reflection.

LEFT: The main courtyard of the Casa Santa Maria. The stone statue of Our Lady of the Immaculate Conception was donated by Archbishop Gaetano Bedini, Apostolic Legate to the United States under Pope Pius IX.

BELOW: The Men of the Casa (front to back, left to right): Rev. Jesus Del Angel, Rev. Gregory Kelly, Rev. Thomas Petro, Rev. Vinh Luu, Rev. Jaimes Ponce, Rev. Joseph Hurtuk, Rev. Pedro Espinoza, Rev. Francis Macatangay, Rev. Thomas Kuns, Rev. Bich Nguyen, Rev. Thomas Urban, Rev. Dean Perri, Rev. John Crowley, Rev. Robert Young, Msgr. Daniel Mueggenborg, Msgr. Francis Kelly, Msgr. James Checchio, Msgr. John Dewane, Msgr. Roger Roensch, Rev. Balappa Selvaraj, Rev. Damian Hills, Rev. Minh Cong Phan, Rev. Timothy Laboe, Rev. Miroslav Vidovic, Rev. Tait Schroeder, Rev. Richard McDonald, Rev. David Barrett, Rev. Jose Maria Cabrera, Rev. Scott Deeley, Rev. Elias Carr, Rev. Avram Brown, Rev. James Bartoloma, Rev. Michael Wurtz, CSC, Rev. Georges DeLaire, Rev. Anthony Robbie, Rev. Brian Clarke, Rev. Gregory Reichlen, Rev. Justin Wachs, Rev. Thinh Duc Pham, Rev. Tim Peters, Rev. Cuong Pham, Rev. Robert Mucci, Rev. James DeViese, Rev. Joshua Guillory, Rev. Denis Heames, Rev. David Carter, Rev. Gerald Goodrum, Rev. Derek Sakowski, Rev. Jeremiah Payne, Rev. Derek Covert, Rev. Mark Ott, Rev. James Rafferty, Rev. William Anton, Rev. Aaron Nord, Rev. Robert Horihan, Rev. Jeffrey Kirby, Rev. Gerard Battersby, Rev. Lawrence Kozak, Rev. Adam Rust, Rev. Carter Griffin, Rev. Richard Donohoe, Rev. Marek Duran, Rev. William Slattery, Rev. Eric Fasano, Rev. Robert Sinatra, Rev. Philip Tangorra, Rev. Peter Groody, Rev. Sean Kilcawley, Rev. Angel Perez Lopez, Rev. Mariusz Stefanowski, Rev. David Pignato, Rev. Alejandro del Bosque, Rev. Anthony Denton, Rev. Dario Miranda, Rev. Edward Becker, Rev. James O'Kane, Rev. Joseph Illo, Rev. Matthew Kauth, Rev. Sergio Lopez, Rev. Slavomir Szkredka

Left: The Degheri Family Library at the Casa Santa Maria contains more than 18,000 volumes and 85 specialized periodicals to assist its student priests and seminarians with their research.

Below Right: The new seminary library on the Janiculum, named after Brother Randal Riede, C.F.X., boasts over 79,000 volumes, being the largest English theological library in all of Europe. Many seminarians use the library as their primary place of study.

Below Left: The Hans Jakob and Ingela Gram Rare Books Room at the Casa library. The beautifully finished woodwork dates to the 18th century, and houses many tomes of theological treatises as well as early volumes of canon law. The collection's oldest work is a copy of *Gratian's Decrees* dating from 1548.

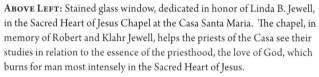

ABOVE LEFT: Stained glass window, dedicated in honor of Linda B. Jewell, in the Sacred Heart of Jesus Chapel at the Casa Santa Maria. The chapel, in memory of Robert and Klahr Jewell, helps the priests of the Casa see their studies in relation to the essence of the priesthood, the love of God, which burns for man most intensely in the Sacred Heart of Jesus.

ABOVE RIGHT: The Eastern Rite Chapel at the Casa Santa Maria allows priests of the various Eastern Rites to offer the Sacred Liturgy in a worthy manner.

RIGHT: The Saint Katherine Drexel and Blessed Kateri Tekakwitha Chapel, donated in 2000 by the Bureau of Catholic Indian Missions, offers another space for prayer.

PAGE 30: The main chapel of the Casa Santa Maria. Both the architecture and art of the chapel date to the 1600s. A 19th century copy of *Our Lady of Mercy*, known affectionately to Casa residents as *Our Lady of Humility*, donated by Archbishop Bedini, hangs above the high altar. The original image, attributed to the Renaissance master Perugino, disappeared sometime in the early 1800s during Napoleon's suppression of monasteries and convents in Rome.

RIGHT: Student priests of the Casa Santa Maria concelebrate Mass in the main chapel.

BELOW RIGHT: The organ itself has become a part of the living memory of the North American College, as it has been used to mark the most important events in the life of the institution. Pictured here is the inscription recording the last High Mass celebrated at the seminary before the move to the Janiculum. This tradition of marking important dates has continued in the new seminary, although no longer on the organ itself. Now the dates and events are etched on the walls leading up to the choir loft.

BELOW LEFT: Console of the organ at the Casa Santa Maria. The organ, purchased in 1867, has been restored several times throughout the many years of its use. It continues to serve as the principal instrument of the Casa chapel.

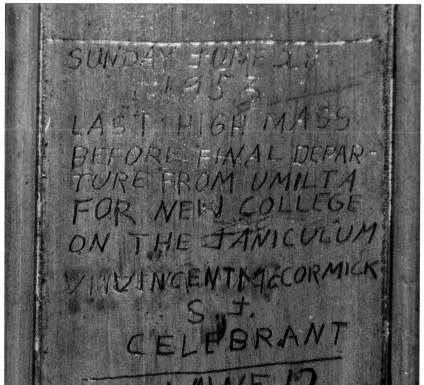

Villa Santa Caterina

The end of each school year brought the seminarians a welcomed change of scenery. Summer months were spent in the picturesque Roman countryside, where the students were afforded time for spiritual renewal. The students made some of their fondest memories during villa season, enjoying a break from their rigorous studies, the chance to travel throughout Italy and ample opportunity to reinforce their bonds of brotherhood.

In its earliest years, the College had used a villa at Grottaferrata for the annual retreat but realized the need for a larger building with more tranquil surroundings. When a reasonable price was asked for a magnificent manor nestled in the Alban hills, Rector William O'Connell immediately sought approval from the Episcopal committee to make the purchase in 1899. The Villa Santa Caterina seemed made-to-order for seminary use, with a spacious landscape, sizeable *palazzo* and chapel. The estate had even belonged to the Orsini family, the very family who had built the original home of the College on Humility Street.

> "SOME OF THE HAPPIEST MEMORIES OF MY LIFE ARE FROM THE DAYS OUT HERE AT THE VILLA! THIS PLACE MADE YOU FEEL LIKE A FAMILY."
>
> -- FRITZ KENNEDY, '40

At the Villa Santa Caterina, the seminarians engaged in sports and recreational activities, put on plays, enhanced their knowledge of European culture, hosted barbecues and were treated to special guest lecturers. An important school tradition was also ushered in at the Villa: the school song, *Ad Multos Annos*, was sung at the closing of each summer session.

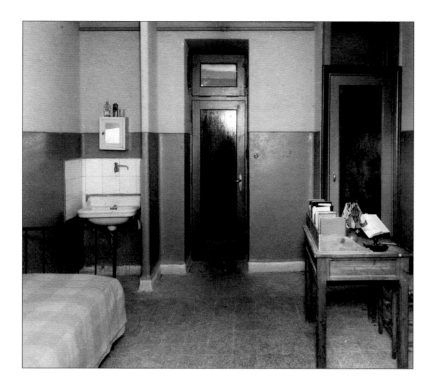

PAGE 32: The seminarians' beloved retreat house, the Villa Santa Caterina.

PAGE 33: Neighborhood children enjoyed the seminarians' visits just as much as the men themselves.

PAGE 34: Villa Santa Caterina chapel.

ABOVE LEFT: Typical seminarian's room used during the stay at the Villa.

ABOVE RIGHT: Seminarians and faculty members celebrate a summer ordination in the Villa Santa Caterina dining room.

RIGHT: Seminarians taking advantage of their summer study break to enjoy a game of billiards.

PAGE 36: Cemetery chapel stands at one of the crossroads inside Campo Verano.

PAGE 37: Simple grave located within Campo Verano. Its tombstone reads, *Io Credo Risorgero* (*I believe I will rise again*).

Campo Verano

In 1874, construction began on a mortuary chapel within the walls of Rome's great cemetery, Campo Verano, for deceased members of the North American College community. The Romanesque memorial mausoleum was finally completed in 1903 on the same grounds where Saints Lawrence, Stephen and Justin lay at rest.

The mausoleum was built with three stories, one dedicated to the College students, one to faculty and one to employees. It was to remain a site of hallowed devotion, forever reminding the seminarians to pray for those who had gone before them in this life.

For decades, the New Men have visited Campo Verano and the College mausoleum in their very first weeks in the Eternal City. Mass has also been traditionally celebrated at its chapel altar on All Souls' Day.

PAGE 38: Sanctuary of the Basilica of St. Lawrence, a Roman deacon and martyr, which sits at the entrance to Campo Verano.

ABOVE LEFT: Exterior view of the North American College mausoleum.

ABOVE RIGHT: Interior of the mausoleum where deceased students, faculty and employees of the College lay at rest.

RIGHT: Tomb of Servant of God, Francis J. Parater, a North American College seminarian.

PAGE 40: Francis J. Parater, October 10, 1897 - February 7, 1920.

PAGE 41: Frank was ever studious during his days at the Xaverian Brother's School and altar boy at Monastery of the Visitation in Richmond.

PAGE 42: View of the Vatican from the top of the Janiculum Hill campus.

PAGE 43: The College was able to realize its expansion plans due to the assistance of Pope Pius XI.

FRANCISCVS J. PARATER

ALVMNVS DIOCESIS RICHMONDIENSIS

OBIIT DIE VII FEBRVARII MCMXX

AETATIS SVAE XXII

Servant of God Francis Parater

The cause for canonization has been officially opened for one North American College seminarian, Francis J. Parater. Born October 10, 1897 in Richmond, Virginia, Frank devoted even the earliest years of his life to the Lord. He was an enthusiastic and bright young man, serving as an altar boy and Boy Scout. His exemplary involvement with the Scouts earned him the rank of Eagle. He graduated from high school as valedictorian in 1917 and entered the college seminary at Belmont Abbey in North Carolina. Two years later, Bishop Denis O'Connell, a former Rector of the North American College, sent Frank to the College in Rome to complete his studies. Frank was instantly popular among his fellow seminarians, displaying warmth, optimism and cheer as he continued on his spiritual journey. Frank's strong sense of piety quickly became known, and he often spoke about what a great privilege it would be to die and be buried in a city made holy by the blood of martyrs.

In late January 1920, Frank fell suddenly ill with rheumatic fever. Confined to his bed and told that his illness was possibly fatal, Frank expressed his desire to get up and kneel on the floor to receive Holy Communion as Viaticum. He was advised

> "...THERE WILL APPEAR FROM TIME TO TIME, A PERSON WHOSE HOLINESS TENDS TO THE HEROIC."
>
> -- FR. ROBERT MCNAMARA, '36

against these wishes and instead knelt on his bed to receive his last Holy Communion. Frank Parater died on February 7, 1920, just months after his arrival in Rome. He was buried in the College mausoleum at Campo Verano.

The untimely passing of this gifted seminarian shocked and saddened the entire North American College community. But spiritual consolation soon came with the discovery of a document entitled, "My Last Will," written by Parater just weeks before his illness. As part of this statement, he writes, *"Death is not unpleasant to me but the most beautiful and welcome event of my life. Death is the messenger of God come to tell us that that our novitiate is ended and to welcome us to the real life … since I was a child I have desired to die for the love of God and for my fellow man…"*

Plans to Expand

Enrollment at the North American College continued to climb in the 1920s, leading the administration to believe that the Humility Street house would soon prove inadequate. Plans to expand the College began, and Rector Charles O'Hern set about to look for fitting property.

Meanwhile, a Methodist minister, Dr. Bertram Tipple, was attempting to build a "counter Vatican" atop Rome's Monte Mario, which was to tower 200 feet above St. Peter's Basilica. While the Italian government ruled against Dr. Tipple's plans, fears arose that another anti-Catholic group may try to realize similar goals above another property for sale on the south side of the Vatican, the Janiculum Hill.

The northern summit of the Janiculum Hill spanned 26 acres and was the former estate of the Gabrielli family. It was too large for the North American College to purchase alone, and the Province of Rome would not agree to sell only a portion of the land. Luckily, the Urban College also happened to be looking for new land on which to expand; the Vatican authorities therefore suggested both colleges complete the deal together.

The American Bishops agreed to pay $600,000 for ten acres of land on the Janiculum Hill. The deal was finalized in 1926, securing the historic Villa Gabrielli and the land for the future seminary of the North American College.

The College Braves World War II

The threat of a second world war loomed over Europe during the late 1930s. Despite Rector Bishop Ralph Hayes' hopes to keep the seminary open, the American consulate ordered that all United States citizens return home without delay. On May 31, 1940, the seminarians donned the civilian clothes they kept in reserve and boarded buses headed to the Port of Genoa.

While World War II raged on, the Humility Street building was home to approximately 300 orphaned boys, while the Janiculum property housed refugees (including several Jewish families, due to its extraterritorial status as part of Vatican City State) and their horses, cows and sheep. The Villa Santa Caterina provided refuge for hundreds of orphaned girls.

In the year of final victory, plans got underway to reopen the College; but debate ensued as to whether operations should recommence at the Humility Street or new Janiculum property. In 1947, the new Rector, Bishop Martin J. O'Connor, presented the College board with a three-fold plan to reestablish the seminary, which included construction on the Janiculum Hill for the new College; renovation of the Humility Street property to serve as a house for graduate student priests; and restoration of the Villa Santa Caterina to house the seminarians until the College's reopening on the Hill. The plan won the bishops' approval and was put into action.

The North American College officially reopened on October 15, 1948, after eight years of suspended activity. Forty-eight newcomers, reverentially called the "Pioneers," quickly reinstated the time-revered traditions so integral to College life, exemplifying the deep dedication and love that all students, whether past or present, held for the seminary.

The House on the Janiculum

Financial hardships and political unrest had postponed construction on the new College for nearly three decades. The impressive campus was at last completed in 1953, serving as an oasis in the chaotic city of Rome. Count Enrico Pietro Galeazzi, the architect of the Sacred Apostolic Palaces, designed the House on the Janiculum with a rich simplicity to coincide with the Roman environment of discipline, study and recollection. The chaste grandeur was carried over to the design of the campus chapel, which included a striking mosaic of the Immaculate Conception on the apse wall. Sitting quite literally in the shadows of St. Peter's Basilica, the campus boasted green space, trees and sports facilities. Forty-eight orange trees dotted the outline of the *cortile* to represent the United States as it existed that year.

"ITS COMPLETION LIGHTS A STRONGER FLAME OF HOPE FOR THE CHURCH IN THE UNITED STATES OF AMERICA AND IN THE WORLD."

-- POPE PIUS XII, ON THE OCCASION OF THE DEDICATION OF THE NEW CAMPUS

With the opening of the new seminary, the newly renovated property on Humility Street became the Casa Santa Maria, the new home of the College's graduate department.

The Janiculum Hill campus was officially dedicated on October 14, 1953. Pope Pius XII accepted Rector Bishop O'Connor's invitation to participate in the joyous celebration and blessed the building in person. The Holy Father was joined by 15 cardinals, six archbishops and 24 bishops who also visited the campus that day to witness its inauguration.

PAGE 44: The first of the "Pioneers" arrive in Rome on March 1, 1948, to reopen the seminary following the Second World War.

PAGE 45: Much damage was inflicted upon the Humility Street property while housing orphaned teenage boys during the war.

PAGE 46: The majestic new campus of the North American College atop the Janiculum Hill.

PAGE 47: A symbol of the seminary's devotion to the Blessed Mother, this statue stands outside one of the College's main entrances.

PAGE 48: Count Enrico Galeazzi's final design for the new College. Described by Pius XII as "*large, majestic, and severe,*" the design was intended to accord with the daily rhythm of the seminary, "*simple and harmonized in the Roman environment of discipline, study, and recollection,*" to use the words of the architect himself.

ABOVE: The second design submitted sought to imitate a Baroque palace, similar to the elegant villas already popular on the Janiculum, especially the 16th century Villa Gabrielli, still present on the College's new property.

LEFT: The earliest design represented a Neoclassical rotunda, reminiscent of the Colosseum.

LEFT AND BELOW: On October 18, 1948, the first Rector of the new college, Bishop Martin J. O'Connor, breaks ground on the new seminary as the architect, Count Enrico Pietro Galeazzi (pictured second from right), looks on. Galeazzi himself held the title of *Architect of the Sacred Apostolic Palaces*.

ABOVE AND RIGHT: The building begins to take shape as construction progresses. The new college, built to house over 300 seminarians in single rooms, included a beautiful sports field, tennis, basketball and handball courts, and eventually acquired a two-lane bowling alley from Pope John XXIII, which he thought the young Americans might enjoy.

Page 52: Completed in only five years, the new seminary sits atop the Janiculum Hill overlooking Vatican City.

Right: Visiting prelates and guests of honor crowd the newly finished Chapel of the Immaculate Conception for its dedication by Pius XII on October 14, 1953.

Below: Kneeling before the altar, Pius XII offers the prayers of dedication for the Chapel of the Immaculate Conception, the heart of the new seminary. In his address to the seminarians on that day, in a world that looked vastly different from Pius IX's day, the Holy Father offered, *"Imprisonment and martyrdom do not loom on the horizons that spread before your eyes… but the Church militant is one body with one Spirit… and that Spirit calls for more than a dash of heroism in every priest worthy of the name…"*

Above: View of the back side of the House on the Janiculum.

Left: The College campus includes a new athletic field, home of the North American Martyrs soccer team.

Left: A view of the western façade of the seminary. Jutting out above the refectory windows is the façade of the main chapel.

Below Right: A California Redwood, planted by Pope John Paul II during his 1980 visit to the College, now towers over its main entrance, which leads directly into the Chapel of the Immaculate Conception.

Below Left: A statue of St. Peter stands facing the College, symbolizing love and filial devotion to the Vicar of Christ on earth. On the statue are inscribed the words of St. Ambrose, *Where Peter is there is the Church, where the Church is there death is not, but eternal life.* The inscription on the portico across from the statue reads, *The young men who have come here from the distant shores of America, looking upon the Vatican Hill, strengthen their faith and their love for the Roman Pontiff.*

Page 56, Right and Below: The *Cortile degli Aranci* boasts 48 orange trees, symbolic of every state in the Union at the time the new campus was dedicated. These orange trees also express a unity with the Casa Santa Maria, whose first inhabitants, the Dominican Sisters, planted orange trees in the belief that St. Dominic brought the first orange grove to Italy.

LEFT: A seminarian's room as it appeared in 1953.

BELOW: Many a meal has been shared in the O'Toole Refectory, where the students strengthen bonds of fraternity.

LEFT: The corridor leading into the Chapel of the Immaculate Conception.

ABOVE: Main doors of the Chapel which read, *Enter into the Temple of God Attentively, Piously and Devotedly.*

PAGE 60: The Chapel of the Immaculate Conception. The community's day begins at 6:15 am with the recitation of Morning Prayer, followed by Holy Mass. The community once again gathers for the communal recitation of Evening Prayer at 6:45 pm. Throughout the day, optional devotional practices are offered in the Chapel of the Immaculate Conception, including the daily Rosary and hour of Eucharistic Adoration.

ABOVE: Bishop William Callahan, OFM. Conv., former spiritual director at the College, offers the Eucharistic Sacrifice during the Easter Vigil, 2008. The most solemn celebration of the entire liturgical year, the Easter Vigil commemorates the Resurrection of Christ from the dead. As the history of Salvation is traced in the readings of the Mass and the Eucharist is offered, the Seminary community is ever more aware of its mission to live in the glory of the Resurrection and to preach the Gospel to those who still *walk in darkness and the shadow of death.*

LEFT: Pope John Paul II offers Mass in the Chapel of the Immaculate Conception during his visit to the College on February 22, 1980, the Feast of the Chair of St. Peter, coincidentally the birthday of the first president of the United States, George Washington. In his homily, the Holy Father urged the seminarians to *"be men of strong faith, who through the Eucharist, the Liturgy of the Hours and daily personal prayer maintain a vibrant friendship with Jesus... your first thoughts must go to Him who is the Christ, the Messiah, the Son of the living God."*

LEFT AND ABOVE: Mosaic of Our Lady of the Immaculate Conception, patroness of the College. Created by Pietro Gaudenzi, the image portrays the purity, tenderness and nobility of Our Lady. Surrounded by courts of angels, the serene Mother daily comforts and intercedes for her sons who gaze upon her in this chapel.

Left: Mosaics at the base of the image of Our Lady of the Immaculate Conception depict four exemplary priests in the history of the Church. Saint Vincent de Paul (far left), Pope St. Gregory the Great (inside left), Pope St. Pius X (inside right) and St. John Vianney (far right).

Below Right: The walls of the sanctuary are covered in frescos by the Roman artists Pio and Silvio Eroli, depicting scenes from the Life of Christ as well as the Joyful Mysteries of the Rosary, here the Annunciation.

Below Left: *Reredos* of the original high altar. The artist, Giuseppe Persichetti, sculpted the frontispiece with the Multiplication of the Loaves from Mark's Gospel as the subject. Christ is seated blessing the people while the Apostles distribute the loaves to the crowd. The fourth adult person from the right is a self-depiction of the artist wearing simple modern clothing. The crucifix and six large geometrically-shaped candlesticks are of gilded bronze, also works of Persichetti. The inscription across the altar reads, *To the Mothers of the Sons of Alma Mater*. The altar itself was consecrated on May 6, 1954, by His Eminence Joseph Cardinal Pizzardo, then Cardinal-Protector of the College.

PAGE 64: Mosaic of the Resurrection of Christ by Pietro Gaudenzi, located at the Galeazzi Altar in the Assumption Chapel. Count Enrico Galeazzi, architect of the College's new campus on the Janiculum, is buried next to this altar. Here, aided by the prayers of the seminary that he built, he awaits the Resurrection.

LEFT AND BELOW: The Casa O'Toole (formerly Casa San Giovanni) has served a varied and noble purpose throughout the years. Erected in 1748 as the *palazzo* of the Villa Gabrielli, the building was used as a house for the poor in the 1800s, housed graduate student priests in the 1930s, and served as a base for caring for refugees living on the property during World War II. These refugees included Roman Jews and American medical students. In 1953, with the opening of the new campus, the house became a convent for the sisters who helped staff the College. In 2008, renovations began to restore and alter the facilities to accommodate the many priests who participate in the Institute for Continuing Theological Education.

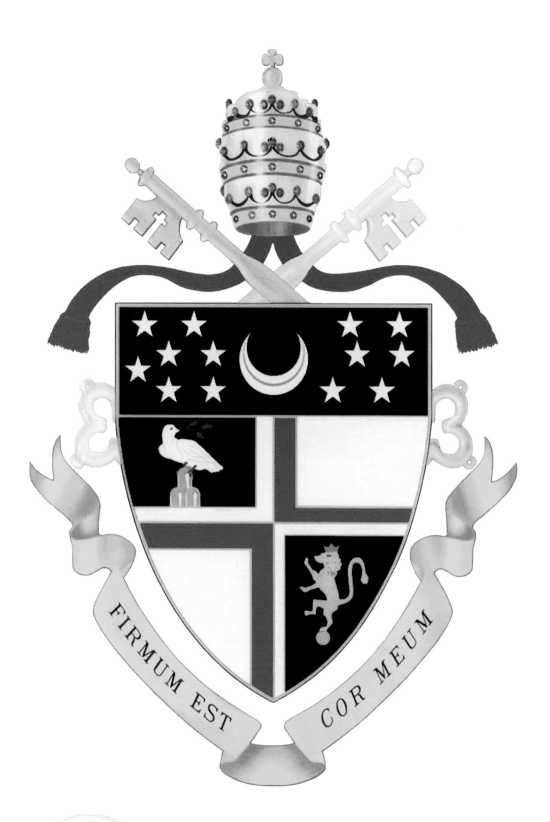

FIRMUM EST COR MEUM

The College Coat of Arms

The coat of arms of the Pontifical North American College was designed by the Most Reverend James H. Griffiths, S.T.D., titular bishop of Gaza and auxiliary to the archbishop of New York, His Eminence Francis Cardinal Spellman, with the collaboration of Mr. William F. G. Ryan. It was executed by Paolo Medici & Figlio Marmorari Romani in 1953.

The primary patroness of the Pontifical North American College is the Immaculate Conception, also the patroness of the United States. The colors are those associated with Our Lady and the United States, blue, silver, and white. The crescent moon, symbol of the Immaculate Conception, is displayed on a blue chief between thirteen silver stars. The scriptural basis of the emblem is Rev. 12:1. The cross is emblazoned in silver and red, paralleling the stripes in the American flag. Pius IX is considered the founder of the original College in 1859 and Pius XII is considered the founder of the present location of the Seminary building. The rampant lion refers to the coat of arms of Blessed Pius IX, the founder of the College on the via dell' Umiltà; the dove with the olive branch refers to that of Pope Pius XII, the founder of the new College on the Janiculum Hill in 1953.

The crest with the papal tiara above two crossed keys testifies that this is a Pontifical Institution as declared by Pope Leo XII on October 25, 1884. The motto of the College *Firmum Est Cor Meum* – "My heart is steadfast" – is taken from the first verse of Psalm 108.

ABOVE: Mantle with bust of the College's founder, Pius IX, in the Red Room of the Casa Santa Maria. Above the statue is the College's Coat of Arms with the motto, *Firmum Est Cor Meum*. At the top is an image of Our Lady of the Immaculate Conception with the Coats of Arms of the College's two Founders, Pius IX (above) and Pius XII (below).

RIGHT: The College Coat of Arms in marble. This marble rendition of the Coat of Arms greets those who enter the building through the east entrance, which has been dubbed by the students simply *Firmum Est*.

PAGE 68: Participants of the S'09 Institute for Continuing Theological Education (ICTE). One of the privileges of the program is the chance to walk with the saints in pilgrimage and to offer Mass in the many Basilicas of Rome. Here the priests find themselves in the Papal Basilica of St. Paul Outside the Walls before a crucifix which spoke to St. Bridget of Sweden in 1370, urging her to found a religious community.

PAGE 69: ICTE S'09 participants standing in front of St. Peter's Basilica. The sabbatical program offers the priests the chance to deepen their theological study in the heart of the Universal Church, close to the tomb of the *Prince of the Apostles*, St. Peter.

Vatican II and Ongoing Priestly Formation

When the Second Vatican Council called for the renewal of priests, the College answered with the founding of the Institute for Continuing Theological Education (ICTE). The sabbatical program has assisted bishops and religious superiors in the ongoing formation of their priests since 1970, enabling them to receive updating in the sacred sciences and return revitalized to their ministries in the United States and elsewhere. Seasoned priests and current seminarians alike have much to gain from living alongside one another during the weeks-long duration of the ICTE program: the students glean a wealth of wisdom from lessons learned in the parishes; the priests see up close and personal the bright future of the Catholic Church.

The historic events of the Council, combined with the growing availability of international air travel, brought more and more American visitors to Rome. Rector Bishop James Hickey established a new office at the College to "turn tourists and visitors into pilgrims" and incite deeper faith experiences for the guests. The Bishop's Office for United States Visitors to the Vatican continues to enhance visits in the Eternal City for more than 60,000 American pilgrims every year. The guests are welcomed and served by a staff of priests, Sisters of Mercy and student seminarians who provide tickets to papal audiences and guided tours of St. Peter's Basilica.

> "IT'S OUR PRIVILEGE TO HELP YOUNG MEN COMING FROM AMERICA TO ROME WITH INVITATIONS FOR PAPAL MASSES, PAPAL AUDIENCES AND OTHER PAPAL EVENTS TO HELP STRENGTHEN THEIR FAITH AND THEIR LOVE OF THE HOLY FATHER."
>
> -- MSGR. ROGER ROENSCH, '58 DIRECTOR
> BISHOPS' OFFICE FOR UNITED STATES VISITORS TO THE VATICAN

College Life Today

A deep spirit of brotherhood is a hallmark of the North American College. The shared spiritual mission and far distance from family, friends and home forge a powerful sense of camaraderie between the men.

Together they take part in prayer, meals, study, holiday celebrations, sporting events and recreational activities, strengthening the foundation they may call upon throughout their future years of pastoral ministry.

"The experience is life-changing. The loyalty is deep and the brotherhood is intimate and life-giving. The joy of the priesthood is very much alive in both houses."

-- Fr. Joseph Fonti, '92, C'98 (Diocese of Brooklyn)

"Our Lord said, 'If you give up home and family, then you will receive a hundred-fold in this life.' I think the bond and brotherhood that priests and seminarians experience with each other is part of that hundred-fold."

-- Fr. Carter Griffin, '04, C'10 (Archdiocese of Washington)

"The College has provided me with the perfect environment to develop friendships that will support me in my future priestly ministry. We know we are never alone because we always have our brothers praying with us."

-- Philip Smith, '11 (Diocese of Toledo)

PAGE 70: In 2008, the College completely renovated the Campo Sportivo with state-of-the-art astro-turf. The Kardos Family Campo Sportivo offers the perfect setting for baseball, soccer and football, and also includes a track around its perimeter. Here Archbishop Michael Sheehan (Archdiocese of Santa Fe) poses with Dishan Candappa (Archdiocese of Melbourne, right), Roberto Ortiz (Archdiocese of Newark, left) and William Brunner (Diocese of Green Bay, back left), after having just blessed the new field.

PAGE 71: Seminarians on the basketball court.

PAGE 72: Kenneth St. Hilaire (Diocese of Spokane) and Justin Wachs (Diocese of Sioux Falls), offer a piano concert in the Red Room for the faculty and students.

LEFT: The College's Pep-Band provides entertainment during the annual Spaghetti Bowl.

BELOW: Students and faculty take to the stage in the annual *New Man/Old Man* Show. Banter between New Men and Old Men as well as students and faculty offers a humorous backdrop to everyday life at the College.

LEFT: Ryan Bredemeyer (Diocese of Peoria) in the St. Joseph Wood Shop. Students use their talents to work on various projects, some even crafting their own furniture.

ABOVE: The Gregory and Linda Jewell student lounge provides plenty of opportunity for recreation and relaxation.

LEFT: Seminarians enjoy a barbecue.

BELOW: John McDonald (Diocese of Birmingham) takes advantage of the Mulva Family Student Kitchen on the 5th floor. Students may sign out the kitchen to prepare meals for groups of friends and visitors.

PAGE 76: The College remains true to its American heritage during its annual Thanksgiving Day feast. Faculty, students and guests sit according to home state. Pictured here are faculty and students from the states of Washington and Oregon.

ABOVE: Peter Finney (Archdiocese of New Orleans) waits on tables during a banquet. Each day, led by the deacons, the students take turns serving lunch to the community.

RIGHT: Joshua Stevens (Diocese of Wheeling-Charleston) brings a slice of American tradition to Rome.

Above: Lively athletic competitions take place at the College. The North American Martyrs soccer team practices and scrimmages often.

Left: Seminarians make up the College's loyal fan base and help to cheer the Martyrs on to victory.

Right: Led by Victor Ingalls and James Morrison (Archdiocese of Mobile), the Martyrs raise their arms in triumph after a win. Each year the various seminaries and colleges in Rome compete in a soccer tournament, the Clericus Cup. The Martyrs have proven strong, making the playoffs every year and winning the semifinals in 2009.

Below: The College's annual Spaghetti Bowl flag football game, the most anticipated game of the year, pits the New Men against the Old Men.

PAGE 80: Fr. James Lease (Diocese of Harrisburg), Fr. Carl Bissinger (Diocese of Fall River) and Fr. Avelino Gonzalez (Archdiocese of Washington) study the Sacred Scriptures. The academic formation is based on a two-cycle system. In First Cycle, students study theology in its various aspects at the Pontifical Universities as an integral whole. In Second Cycle, students focus on one particular branch of theology for a specialized degree. That might include Sacred Scripture, Dogmatic Theology, Fundamental Theology, Liturgical Theology, Moral Theology and the other Ecclesiastical Disciplines such as Church History, Canon Law and Sacred Music.

LEFT: Seminarians take part in a Pastoral Counseling Workshop led by Dr. Susanne Harvath, a noted counselor from the Archdiocese of Saint Louis. Each year, before classes begin, students are required to participate in various seminars and workshops covering many important topics related to priestly life and ministry. These intensive courses on the Liturgy, preaching, counseling, the human virtues and the principles of the spiritual life are all continued by means of weekly meetings throughout the year. Over four years, the students deepen their knowledge and integration of what John Paul II deemed the Four Pillars of Priestly Formation: human, spiritual, intellectual and pastoral.

BELOW: Archbishop J. Augustine DiNoia, O.P. delivers the annual Carl J. Peter Lecture in 2008. The Chair of Homiletics at the College is named after Rev. Carl J. Peter, a priest from the Archdiocese of Omaha, noted for his preaching skills. In his lecture, the Archbishop engaged the community in a lively talk about how to preach well to young adults today. He invited all present to consider how a modern audience could reasonably reflect on some of the unpopular claims that Christianity must make in the modern world. First, the fact that God has definitively sought man out in Jesus Christ, the sole mediator of salvation. Next, the claim that in conforming one's life to Christ through faith, human authenticity and freedom are not suppressed, but rather fully realized. Finally, he reflected on the fact that the moral law of Christ, far from being legalistic, leads to the fulfillment and sanctification of our desires.

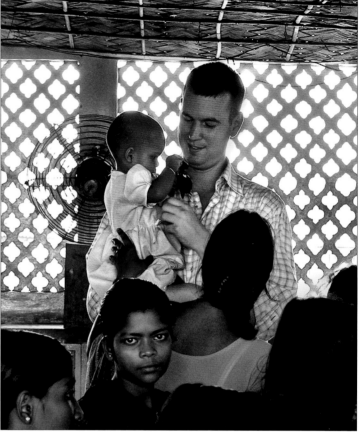

Above Left and Above Right: Andrew Roza (Archdiocese of Omaha, pictured above left) and Peter Purpura (Diocese of Brooklyn, pictured above right) engage the youth during a mission trip to India, sponsored by Catholic Relief Services.

Left: Fr. Brendan Lally, S.J. and seminarian Neal Hock (Diocese of Grand Island) at the Santa Luisa School in San Salvador. Each year the College sponsors a trip to El Salvador as a way for the seminarians to immerse themselves in a cultural and ecclesial experience not typically their own. The students are exposed to the Church as She exists in Central America and seek to deepen their own faith through the encounter with a culture rich in faith, yet poor in material goods.

RIGHT: A seminarian takes in the sunset over the Sea of Galilee.

BELOW: Fr. David Songy, O.F.M. Cap. offers Mass at an outdoor shrine in Assisi for the New Men in 2008. Each year the New Men spend a weekend on retreat together in the peaceful city where Saints Francis and Clare so powerfully experienced the Lord's call to the Faith.

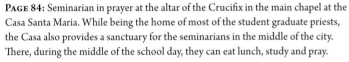

PAGE 84: Seminarian in prayer at the altar of the Crucifix in the main chapel at the Casa Santa Maria. While being the home of most of the student graduate priests, the Casa also provides a sanctuary for the seminarians in the middle of the city. There, during the middle of the school day, they can eat lunch, study and pray.

ABOVE LEFT: Seminarian James Baron (Diocese of Colorado Springs) prays a Rosary while on retreat at Rocca di Papa, outside the city of Rome. Each year, the men take their annual spiritual retreat. The spiritual formation program seeks to impart the principles of the spiritual life to the future priests through liturgical prayer, spiritual conferences, personal spiritual direction, annual retreats and days of recollection.

ABOVE RIGHT: During the Year of St. Paul (2008-2009) seminarians offer prayers at the tomb of St. Paul in the Basilica of St. Paul Outside the Walls in Rome. One of the deepest privileges of studying in Rome is the opportunity to pray at the tombs of the saints and martyrs of the Christian Faith.

RIGHT: The New Men (Class of 2011) kneel in prayer before the tomb of St. Peter. During their time in the Eternal City, the seminarians often visit the Basilica to foster their love and devotion to the leader of the Twelve Apostles, to whom Christ said, *"You are Peter and upon this Rock I will build my Church, and the gates of hell shall not prevail against it"* (Mt. 16:18). As they pray at Peter's tomb, the seminarians also foster their love and loyalty to the successor of Peter, the Holy Father.

ABOVE LEFT: The seminary choir sings at its biannual Christmas concert. The Music Choir sings at all of the solemn Liturgies at the College, including Solemn Mass and Vespers each Sunday. The choir released its first compact disc in 2009 with JAV Recordings, *Regina Immaculata: Mass in Honor of the Immaculate Conception*. Under the direction of Mr. Christopher Berry and accompanied by noted organist Stephen Tharp, the choir recorded the entire Mass for the College's principal feast, the Immaculate Conception, using all of the proper Gregorian antiphons as well as Maurice Durufle's arrangement of the Mass *Cum Jubilo*.

ABOVE RIGHT: Bishop William Callahan, OFM. Conv., former spiritual director at the College, ordains James Adams (Diocese of Kalamazoo) to the Order of Deacon at the Altar of the Chair in St. Peter's Basilica in October 2008.

LEFT: The end of the procession enters the sanctuary for the College's 2008 Diaconate Ordination. Each October, the new class of deacons is ordained at the Altar of the Chair in St. Peter's Basilica. Family and friends come from all over the world to witness their loved ones lay down their lives in service to Christ and His Church. As deacons, the men are conformed to Christ the Servant. They seek to live out His charity through their sacramental and diaconal service, preaching, and commitment to obedience, prayer and celibacy.

LEFT: The new deacons are vested with the stole and dalmatic, the liturgical vestments proper to the deacon.

BELOW LEFT: Pablo Migone (Diocese of Savannah) and James Melnick (Diocese of Little Rock) receive the Book of the Gospels from the bishop with the following exhortation: *Receive the Gospel of Christ, whose herald you now are. Believe what you read, teach what you believe, and practice what you teach.*

BELOW RIGHT: The newly ordained deacons congratulate each other immediately after the ordination. The Second Vatican Council declared that *"the Spirit is, for the Church and for each and every believer, the principle of their union and unity in the teaching of the apostles and fellowship, in the Breaking of Bread and prayer."* Communion and fraternity are essential in the priestly life, but can only be brought about by lives lived in communion with the Triune God, receiving from the Father the image of His Son and the power of His Spirit.

PAGE 88: The newly vested deacons seek to comprehend the powerful reality that they have just entered into.

PAGE 89: A statue of St. Peter stands on the Janiculum campus grounds.

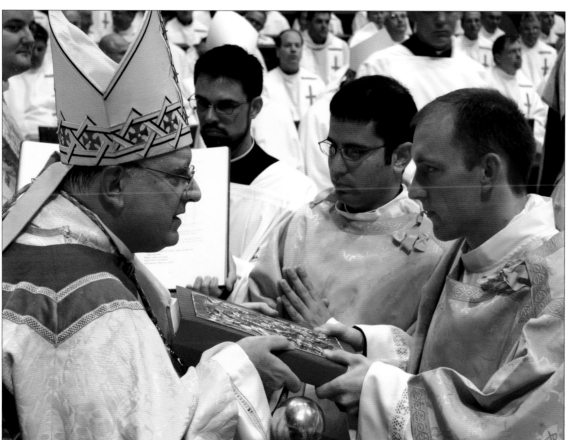

Sent to Preach the Gospel

Generations of men have come to the North American College to be formed after the heart and mind of Jesus Christ. Throughout its 150-year history, the College has prepared more than 3,500 seminarians to be pastors for the people of the United States and other parts of the world.

"WE HAVE A TREMENDOUS AND HUMBLING RESPONSIBILITY. THE CHURCH EXPECTS US TO BE HOLY LEADERS, MEN CHARGED WITH THE TASK OF BRINGING GOD TO THE FAITHFUL AND THE FAITHFUL TO GOD. THERE IS NO DOUBT THAT THE MEN THEMSELVES, TOMORROW'S PRIESTS, ARE THE COLLEGE'S GREATEST AND MOST EXCITING ASSET. IN THIS WAY, THE COLLEGE IS A GENUINE BEACON OF HOPE FOR THE FUTURE."

-- JOHNNY BURNS, '10 (ARCHDIOCESE OF MILWAUKEE)

"ROME CAN PROVIDE A SOLID AND COMPREHENSIVE PREPARATION FOR THE PRIESTHOOD TO THOSE WHO SEEK IT. WE STUDY THE FAITH, HISTORY AND TRADITIONS OF THE CHURCH NOT ONLY FOR OURSELVES. WE STUDY IT TO PASS IT ON TO OTHERS."

-- FR. CARTER GRIFFIN, '04, C '10 (ARCHDIOCESE OF WASHINGTON)

"ROME IS THE FOCAL POINT OF ALL THAT THE CHURCH REPRESENTS. IT'S ALSO A GREAT PLACE OF THEOLOGICAL EDUCATION, WHERE THE GREAT MINDS OF THE CHURCH COME TO TEACH. IT OPENS UP YOUR MIND TO THE WORLD, AND TO BE ABLE TO STUDY IN THE MIDDLE OF ALL THIS IS A GREAT BLESSING."

-- MSGR. ROGER ROENSCH, '58 (ARCHDIOCESE OF WASHINGTON)

CLASS OF 1860

Edward McGlynn (New York)

CLASS OF 1862

Maurice Brann (Newark)

CLASS OF 1863

Michael Corrigan (Newark), Anthony Gingsheim (Alton), Patrick Hennessy (Newark), James Nilan (New York), Ambrose O'Neil (Albany), Daniel O'Regan (Cincinnati), Patrick Ward (Pittsburgh)

CLASS OF 1864

Edward Fitzpatrick (Brooklyn), Thomas J. Gardner (Brooklyn), William Hart (Hartford), William Meriwether (Charleston)

CLASS OF 1865

John J. Byrne (Philadelphia), John Cassidy (San Francisco), Ignace F. Horstmann (Philadelphia), James P. Moroney (Philadelphia), Harry A. Northrop (Charleston), Reuben Parsons (New York), Thomas A. Reid (Brooklyn), Joseph Richter (Cincinnati), Patrick Smith (Albany)

CLASS OF 1866

Christopher Hughes (Hartford), John M. Jones (Baltimore), John Kearney (New York), Thomas S. Lee (Baltimore), Charles P. O'Connor (Philadelphia), William Poole (Savannah), Daniel Quigley (Charleston), John Sheridan (Hartford)

CLASS OF 1867

James F. Barry (New York), Thomas Edwards (Chicago), Cornelius McDermott (Philadelphia), John P. Morris (Newark)

CLASS OF 1868

Patrick Garvey (Philadelphia), Charles Gavin (Chicago), Edward Gavin (Chicago), William Kieran (Philadelphia), Anthony Ulrich (Cincinnati), Ernest Van Dyke (Detroit)

CLASS OF 1869

Theodore A. Metcalf (Boston)

CLASS OF 1870

Patrick Cusack (Cincinnati), John Farrelly (New York), Peter Geyer (Cincinnati), Alexander Harnist (Louisville), Charles O'Keeffe (New York)

▶ CLASS OF 1871

John Nugent (San Francisco), Charles O'Keefe (New York), Francis McCarthy (Pittsburgh), John Raber (Brooklyn)

◀ CLASS OF 1872

F. Patrick Fitzmaurice (Philadelphia), David Hayes (St. Louis), Benjamin Kelly (Wilmington), Henry Moeller (Cincinnati), James Sinnott (Philadelphia)

CLASS OF 1873

Owen Corrigan (Baltimore), David Doherty (St. Louis), William Harty (Hartford), Louis Hostlot (New York), Andrew Hynes (St. Louis), Daniel Jones (Natchez), James McGeveran (Philadelphia), Frederick Schonhoff (Cincinnati), John B. Smith (Boston)

CLASS OF 1874

John F. Brummer (Cincinnati), Michael Gleeson (St. Louis), John Longhran (Brooklyn), Thomas Maharf (Cleveland), James McDonald (Boston), John Schandel (Newark)

CLASS OF 1875

Michael Brennan (Newark), Maurice Burke (Chicago), Andrew Byrne (St. Paul), James Curran (New York), Patrick F. Fitzmaurice (Philadelphia), Michael Holland (Newark), Cornelius Mahony (New York)

CLASS OF 1876

Bernard Clarke (Buffalo), Henry Moeller (Cincinnati), James Sinnott (Philadelphia), John Woods (New York)

CLASS OF 1877

Edward Conroy (New York), Eugene Donnelly (Brooklyn), Denis O'Connell (Richmond), Joseph O'Keefe (Scranton), Charles F. Payten (New York)

CLASS OF 1878

Edward Brady (Wilmington), John E. Burke (New York), Hugh McDevitt (Cincinnati), Charles McDonnell (New York)

CLASS OF 1879

John McElhinny (New York)

CLASS OF 1880

William Daly (Philadelphia), William Degnan (New York), John Farrelly (Nashville), Michael Hoban (Scranton), John H. May (St. Louis), Joseph A. Testes (Cleveland)

CLASS OF 1881

Hugh P. Gallagher (San Francisco), Henry Kuenner (St. Louis), Jeremy Sullivan (Newark)

CLASS OF 1882

James M. Connelly (Baltimore), James Howard (Alton), Joseph A. Maher (New York), Edward McGoldrick (Brooklyn), Daniel O'Toole (Newark), George Reis (St. Louis), August J. Schulte (Philadelphia), Thomas J. Shahan (Hartford)

CLASS OF 1883

Philip J. Carroll (St. Louis), Henry F. Conboy (Providence), James F. Crowley (Brooklyn), James B. Curry (New York), John F. Ford (Boston), William Galvin (Providence), Charles F. Glennen (Boston), Patrick F. Maughan (New York), James F. Talbot (Boston), Edward Tiernay (Richmond), Nicholas R. Walsh (Boston)

CLASS OF 1884

William H. B. Deasy (Boston), Edward L. Kenny (New York), Thomas P. McLaughlin (New York), William O'Connell (Boston), Joseph H. Pohlschneider (Cincinnati), William J. Scott (Wilmington)

CLASS OF 1885

Daniel Cunnion (New York), Thomas S. Duhigg (Brooklyn), Edward J. Hanna (Rochester), Thomas H. Kelly (Albany), Edward Pace (St. Augustine)

CLASS OF 1886

Joseph Bussmann (Cincinnati), John M. Curley (New York), Bernard Duffy (New York), Nevin F. Fisher (Philadelphia), Nathan J. Mooney (Chicago), William G. Payne (Richmond), James Raywood (New York), Michael Riordan (Baltimore)

CLASS OF 1887

James Coffey (St. Louis), Edmund Cronin (New York), John Denny (Pittsburgh), Terence Dolan (Hartford), John Hickey (Cincinnati), Thomas Kennedy (Philadelphia), William Maher (Hartford), Thomas McManus (New York)

▼ CLASS OF 1888

John Shaw (Mobile), Patrick Fitzgerald (Brooklyn), Edward Welsh (Alton), John Stafford (Newark), Maurice Fitzgerald (Brooklyn), Charles Mackel (Newark), William Guinon (New York), Frederick Rooker (Albany), Michael Riordan (Baltimore), Thomas Kennedy (Philadelphia), John J. Sheahan (Buffalo)

CLASS OF 1889

William Degnan (New York), Edward McGoldrick (Brooklyn), Daniel O'Toole (Newark), James B. Conroy (Albany), John J. McGinley (St. Augustine), John Donnelly (Mobile), Edward F. McManus (Buffalo), John L. Keating (New York), Thomas J. Shahan (Hartford)

◄ CLASS OF 1890

FRONT ROW: Dennis Dougherty (Philadelphia), Patrick Supple (Boston), John Barrett (Brooklyn), Patrick McGee (Providence)

SECOND ROW: Henry Newly (New York), John Lennon (New York), William Foley (Springfield, MA), Patrick Mahoney (New York)

CLASS OF 1891 ►

FRONT ROW: Bernard Kuhlman (Cincinnati), Patrick Farrell (Cleveland), George Dougherty (Baltimore)

SECOND ROW: Humphrey Moynahan (St. Paul), James Baxter (Boston), Thomas Walsh (St. Louis), Leo Kuappe (Boston), Henry K. White (San Francisco)

CLASS OF 1892 ▶

Bernard Campbell (Harrisburg), Michael Corcoran (Manchester), James Donovan (Manchester), George Fitzpatrick (Newark), Maurice P. Foley (St. Augustine), Bernard Charles Guendling (Fort Wayne), Patrick Horan (Little Rock), Lucien Johnston (Baltimore), James Kennefic (Richmond), Michael Maher (St. Augustine), William McGinnis (Brooklyn), Thomas U. Moore (St. Augustine), John Morris (Nashville), George Murphy (Cleveland), John O'Brien (St. Augustine)

◀ CLASS OF 1893

Hubert Behr (Newark), Andrew Breen (Rochester), Michael Carroll (Wilmington), Francis Dolan (Boston), Denis Driscoll (New York), Edmund Gibbons (Buffalo), Edward Higney (Providence), Patrick Lennon (New York), Thomas Lynch (Brooklyn), Thomas McGee (Providence), Andrew Meehan (Rochester), Simon Orf (St. Louis), William Plamondon (Burlington), Edmund Shanahan (Boston), William Turner (St. Augustine)

CLASS OF 1894

FRONT ROW: Daniel J. Curley (New York), Edward Keough (Chicago), Robert Fitzgerald (Hartford)

SECOND ROW: James O'Brien (New York), William Donohoe (New York), Emil Wolfstyn (Detroit)

CLASS OF 1895

FRONT ROW: Edward Devlin (Winona), James Kelly (Brooklyn), Paul L. Reynolds (Baltimore), John McGinley (Philadelphia), Francis Lavelle (New York)

SECOND ROW: John Bowen (Chicago), William White (Brooklyn), John Connelly (Wilmington), John Duffy (Philadelphia)

CLASS OF 1896 ▶

FRONT ROW: Emil Gefell (Rochester), Edward Tierney (New York), Michael Nolan (Rochester), Thomas McGrath (Altoona), Bernard Stolte (St. Louis)

SECOND ROW: Charles Smith (Newark), Victor Brueker (Vincennes), James Coyle (Mobile), Michael Henry (Mobile), Dennis Bustin (Scranton), William Temple (Wilmington)

CLASS OF 1897 ▶

FRONT ROW: Cornelius Brennan (Hartford), John Braunan (St. Paul), John Spensley (Albany), Bonaventure Broderick (Hartford), William Creedon (New York), John Cummiskey (Winona)

SECOND ROW: Martin Grasser (New York), Denis L. Gleason (Hartford), Thomas Monehan (Newark), John McLoughlin (Hartford), Leo Gossman (Winona), Francis Ryan (St. Paul)

THIRD ROW: William Glynn (Syracuse), John Ferry (Brooklyn), Patrick C. Gavan (Baltimore), Edmund P. Flaherty (Brooklyn)

CLASS OF 1898 ▶

FRONT ROW: William Sinnott (New York), Rudolph Nickel (Milwaukee), John Zybura (Cleveland), Herman Rechtin (Cincinnati), John O'Toole (Brooklyn), John Norton (Baltimore)

SECOND ROW: Francis O'Bryan (Chicago), Joseph Cruse (St. Louis), James Noonan (St. Augustine), John O'Brien (New York)

◀ CLASS OF 1899

Peter Blessing (Providence), John Driscoll (Providence), Albert Gass (St. Louis), John Grant (Buffalo), James Harley (Chicago), Alexander McKay (Philadelphia), Alexander Mercer (St. Louis), D.J. Murphy (Nashville), Thomas O'Reilley (Cleveland), John Pleus (St. Louis), Edmund J. Wirth (Rochester)

◄ CLASS OF 1900

FRONT ROW: Edward Downes (Hartford), Francis Headon (Chicago), Felix H. O'Neill (Newark), Richard Gillen (New Orleans), Daniel Dever (Philadelphia)

SECOND ROW: Walter Sweeney (Boston), Patrick MacLaughlin (New York), James Veale (St. Augustine), Eugene Donnelly (Brooklyn), James Walsh (Fort Wayne), James Hanrahan (Springfield, MA)

CLASS OF 1901 ►

Daniel Callahan (Newark), John Casey (Springfield, MA), John P. Doyle (Brooklyn), William Flynn (Hartford), William Foran (Springfield, MA), William Garrigan (Philadelphia), William Garrity (Vincennes), James Higgins (Brooklyn), Daniel Kehoe (Philadelphia), U. J. McDonnell (New York), Hugh A. O'Brien (Mobile), Francis O'Hern (Rochester), Patrick O'Reilly (Boston), Frank A. Quinn (Philadelphia), Patrick Reardon (New York), Michael Scanlan (Boston), George J. Smith (Vincennes), Michael Splaine (Boston), Henry Tracey (New York)

Class of 1901

Photo not available.

CLASS OF 1902 ▶

FRONT ROW: William Garrity (Vincennes), William Garrigan (Philadelphia), Daniel Kehoe (Philadelphia), Thomas F. Kennedy (Rector), Michael Splaine (Boston), William Flynn (Hartford)

SECOND ROW: Michael Steines (Syracuse), John J. Toomey (New York), James Comdan (New York), Joseph Joyce (Hartford), Richard Jordan (Scranton), Michael Scanlan (Boston), Francis Goggin (Rochester), Joseph Rummell (New York)

CLASS OF 1903 ▶

FRONT ROW: Stuart Chambers (New York), Michael Steines (Syracuse), Joseph McKenna (Brooklyn), Thomas F. Kennedy (Rector), Lawrence S. Fell (Buffalo), James Dumphy (Springfield, MA), Alfred Roth (Syracuse)

SECOND ROW: John Sheehan (Grand Rapids), Joseph Corrigan (Philadelphia), Nicholas Coleman (Hartford), David Supple (Boston), Joseph Rummel (New York), Leo P. Gaus (St. Cloud)

◄ CLASS OF 1904

FRONT ROW: Charles A. Finn (Boston), John Murphy (Erie), Thomas F. Kennedy (Rector), Bernard Mahoney (Albany), Daniel Tully (Springfield, MA)

SECOND ROW: Michael Mulligan (Newark), Alvah Doran (Philadelphia), John Turner (New York), Edmund Fitzmaurice (Philadelphia), James Bartley (Providence)

THIRD ROW: Martin O'Gara (New York), John Driscoll (Portland)

◄ CLASS OF 1905

FRONT ROW: Joseph Kassman (Cincinnati), John Harty (Brooklyn), Joseph F. Nolan (Cleveland), Thomas F. Kennedy (Rector), Ambrose Dore (Boston), James Talbot (New York), Andrew Brennan (Scranton)

SECOND ROW: Raymond Noll (Indianapolis), Charles McCarthy (Newark), Daniel Mulcahy (Dubuque), James Supple (Boston), Joseph English (St. Louis), John F. Eckenrode (Baltimore), William D. Nugent (St. Louis), John Cooper (Baltimore)

THIRD ROW: John F. Wolfe (Dubuque), James H. McGinnis (New York)

◀ CLASS OF 1906

Augustine Asfaly (New York), Charles Borneman (Philadelphia), George Burthel (New York), James Dougherty (New York), Augustine F. Hickey (Boston), William Higgins (Springfield, MA), Edward Hoar (Brooklyn), John Kelliher (Richmond), John Kieman (Newark), Charles O'Hern (Chicago), Bernard D. Rogers (Chicago), Joseph Schade (Philadelphia), Edward Sinnott (New York)

CLASS OF 1907 ▶

FRONT ROW: Charles Borneman (Philadelphia), Charles O'Hern (Chicago), Augustine Hickey (Boston), Thomas F. Kennedy (Rector), Joseph McGlinchy (Boston), Edward Hoar (Brooklyn), Leo McGinley (Philadelphia)

SECOND ROW: Peter O'Loughlin (Lincoln), Edmund O'Connor (Buffalo), James Moynihan (St. Paul), John Shields (Harrisburg), Joseph Fisch (Sioux City), Joseph Ratto (Philadelphia)

THIRD ROW: John Curran (Boston), Leonard Baluta (Harrisburg), Terence Marshall (New York), Lockley Appo (Brooklyn)

CLASS OF 1908 ▶

FRONT ROW: George Dequoy (Grand Rapids), William Everett (Hartford), Thomas Coakley (Pittsburgh), Thomas F. Kennedy (Rector), John Powers (Boston), William Scullen (Cleveland), Francis Bradley (Providence)

SECOND ROW: John Duffy (Newark), Francis Campbell (New York), James Golden (Scranton), Raphael Kinnane (Cleveland), Alphonsus Smith (Indianapolis), Michael Kerper (Dubuque), Francis Murphy (Boston), Edward Kramer (Cleveland), James Cramey (Dubuque)

THIRD ROW: Aloysius Weber (New York), Joseph McDermott (Philadelphia), William Murphy (Detroit), Marc Driscoll (Boston), James Murphy (Sioux City), Edward Baxter (New York)

Class of 1909

Photo not available.

◀ CLASS OF 1909

Michael Ambrosey (Dubuque), Thomas G. Carroll (New York), Charles Conley (Chicago), John Cox (Scranton), Thomas Deegan (New York), Peter Dooley (St. Louis), Thomas Drennan (Hartford), William Enright (Brooklyn), Richard Gerow (Mobile), Joseph Grant (Wilmington), James Griffin (Chicago), John F. Hardeman (Nashville), Rudolph Hayes (Pittsburgh), Alfred Hyland (Grand Rapids), Edward Jordan (Scranton), William Keefe (Indianapolis), John Lynch (St. Louis), Raphael Markham (Cincinnati), Charles McClellan (Chicago), Edward Mooney (Cleveland), Robert Mulcahey (New York), William Ryder (New York), Henry Walsh (Chicago), Walter Warakomski (Chicago)

◄ CLASS OF 1910

FRONT ROW: James Griffin (Chicago), William Murphy (Chicago), Rudolph Hayes (Pittsburgh), Thomas F. Kennedy (Rector), William Long (Chicago), John Walsh (Scranton), William Enright (Brooklyn)

SECOND ROW: Benedict Gillon (Albany), Joseph Grant (Wilmington), Paul Laskowski (Chicago), Thomas Carroll (New York), William Gill (New York), Louis Tiernan (Kansas City, MO), John Lynch (Wilmington), Francis O'Connor (Louisville)

THIRD ROW: Martin Hayden (Chicago), Samuel Stritch (Nashville), John Smith (Boston), Henry Walsh (Chicago)

◄ CLASS OF 1911

FRONT ROW: John Sonefeld (Grand Rapids), John Ford (Chicago), Thomas Canty (Chicago), Francis Reenan (Brooklyn), Thomas F. Kennedy (Rector), Adolph Bechman (Cincinnati), Paul Drevniak (Chicago), John Lannon (Chicago), Augustine McNeil (St. Joseph)

SECOND ROW: William Rooney (Chicago), Henry Kemper (Chicago), Bernard McNamara (Baltimore), Moses Kiley (Chicago), Cornelius Cronin (Boston), Charles White (Grand Rapids), John Flanagan (Chicago), John Hennessy (Dubuque), Richard Haberlin (Boston), Joseph Murphy (Boston), Andrew O'Brien (Boston)

THIRD ROW: Thomas Carroll (Brooklyn), James Flanagan (Brooklyn), Francis Woods (Brooklyn), Martin Cavanaugh (New York), Francis Walsh (Peoria), Leo Gifford (Boston), Eugene Burke (Newark), James Rogers (Brooklyn), Edward McCarthy (Seattle), Christopher Molloy (Brooklyn), William Adrian (Davenport)

CLASS OF 1912 ▶

FRONT ROW: Harold Tramor (Chicago), Barry O'Toole (Toledo), Michael Corallo (Chicago), John Doody (Chicago), Thomas F. Kennedy (Rector), William McViegh (Baltimore), Maurice Connor (St. Joseph), Thomas Scanlan (Brooklyn), John Mielcarek (Chicago)

SECOND ROW: John Gregroire (Winona), Thomas Kirby (Cleveland), William Kane (Philadelphia), William Moore (Syracuse), Patrick Leahy (Brooklyn), William Rohan (Dubuque), William O'Brien (Boston), Peter Johnson (Milwaukee), Thomas Burke (Newark), Patrick Meagher (Boston), Thomas Connor (Manchester)

THIRD ROW: Frederick Shields (Erie), John Halligan (New York), Michael Costello (Alton), John Lamott (Cincinnati), Francis Ross (Philadelphia), Clarence Murphy (Brooklyn), John Brady (Cleveland), John Henel (Dallas-Ft. Worth)

CLASS OF 1913 ▶

FRONT ROW: Francis Kelly (Winona), James Riordan (St. Augustine), Eugene Sands (Mobile), Charles McAuliffe (New York), Andrew Farrell (Hartford), Thomas F. Kennedy (Rector), George Parker (Chicago), Philip Brennan (Richmond), John Sheridan (New York), William Fischer (St. Louis), Henry Takkenburg (Davenport)

SECOND ROW: Alex Gorski (Chicago), Denis O'Brien (Boston), Thomas Friel (Chicago), James Fallon (Boston), John Culhane (Boston), Stanislaus Bona (Chicago), William Little (New York), Thomas McKay (Philadelphia), Frederick Saunders (Little Rock), Cornelius Hayes (New York)

THIRD ROW: Thomas Deignan (Albany), Thomas McNichols (Chicago), Louis Fitzpatrick (Grand Rapids), Arthur Kiffin (Albany), Francis Magner (Chicago), Francis Broschart (Brooklyn), Stephen Davis (Davenport), Edward Lyons (Philadelphia), William Anthony (Cincinnati)

FOURTH ROW: John Anderson (Hartford), Ignace Wilbur (St. Louis), Angel Zwisler (Cleveland), Ignace McNamee (Portland)

CLASS OF 1914 ▶

FRONT ROW: Richard Brennan (Cleveland), Thomas Normoyle (Winona), James Kelty (Brooklyn), Joseph Breslin (New York), Thomas F. Kennedy (Rector), George Campbell (Oregon City), John Heagan (Cleveland), Francis Garvey (New York), John Martin (Providence)

SECOND ROW: Joseph Mullen (Cleveland), John Kozlowski (Chicago), George Johnson (Toledo), Anthony Lorenz (Dubuque), Leo McNamara (Chicago)

THIRD ROW: Joseph Schaeffner (Brooklyn), Joseph Lee (Wilmington), James Roche (Dubuque), Arthur O'Connell (San Francisco), Daniel Murphy (Chicago), John Mogan (Nashville)

◀ CLASS OF 1915

FRONT ROW: John Kelly (Hartford), Francis Malone (Cleveland), Charles Buddy (St. Joseph), Thomas F. Kennedy (Rector), Louis Kelliher (Boston), Francis Whitely (Boston), James Murray (Chicago)

SECOND ROW: Patrick Geehan (San Antonio), Andrew Kelly (Hartford), Bartholomew Eustace (New York), Ambrose Hennessey (Boston), Frederick Mulry (Boston), Nicholas Jakubowski (Wilmington), James Cronin (Boston), William Conroy (Boston), Thomas Donahue (Davenport)

THIRD ROW: Thomas Nolan (Chicago), John Mullaly (Mobile), Hugh Lamb (Philadelphia), Francis Monaghan (Newark), Michael O'Flynn (Harrisburg), John Mullin (Cheyenne), Joseph Schleck (Buffalo)

◄ CLASS OF 1916

FRONT ROW: Aloysius Flynn (Boston), Paul Smith (Chicago), Francis McCarthy (Chicago), Joseph Harrington (Chicago), Lawrence Killian (Boston), Joseph Berger (Chicago), Most Rev. Thomas F. Kennedy (Rector), Eugene Caulfield (Scranton), Thomas Geraghty (St. Louis), Julius Haun (Winona), Michael V. Holter (Cleveland), Daniel Burke (Boston), Francis Cummings (Boston)

SECOND ROW: Henry Matimore (Chicago), Charles White (Boston), Francis Oechsler (Brooklyn), Francis McConville (Newark), George Petro (Philadelphia), Henry Scharphoff (Dubuque), Francis Spellman (Boston), John Cross (Brooklyn), Anthony Flynn (Philadelphia), George Hegeman (Milwaukee), Joseph Christopher (Rockford), Robert Lucey (Los Angeles)

THIRD ROW: Gerald Bergen (Peoria), Joseph Wehrle (Erie), William Mockenhaupt (Chicago), Edward Quinn (Cincinnati), John Jurasko (Brooklyn), Hamilton Shea (New York)

CLASS OF 1917 ►

FRONT ROW: Philip Mahoney (Chicago), James Halleran (Chicago), Leo Devlin (Winona), James Kenny (Grand Rapids), Charles A. O'Hern (Rector), John Cartwright (Baltimore), Thomas Noa (Grand Rapids), James Kealy (Chicago), John Wagener (Chicago)

SECOND ROW: Albert J. Carmody (Portland), Patrick Kinsella (Brooklyn), Andrew Daley (Springfield, MA), John Phelan (Boston), Charles Dunbury (Boston), Edward Kelly (Baker City), Thomas Killela (Helena), John Bonner (Philadelphia), Garrett Condon (Boston), Francis Bredestege (Cincinnati), Charles McCormack (Albany)

THIRD ROW: John Mahony (Cleveland), Walter Czarnecki (Toledo), Francis Driscoll (Brooklyn), Henry Gross (Los Angeles), Charles Robinson (Nashville), Charles Fitzgerald (New York), John Monaghan (New York)

CLASS OF 1918 ►

FRONT ROW: Jason Grady (Hartford), James Reardon (Grand Rapids), Francis Sallaway (Boston), John Davidson (Cleveland), Thomas Markham (Boston), Charles A. O'Hern (Rector), John Walsh (New York), Francis Burke (Boston), John Curtin (Hartford), Samuel Lucey (Chicago), William O'Brien (Chicago)

SECOND ROW: Jason Walsh (Chicago), William Kelly (Baltimore), Jesse Gatton (Alton), John Bolen (Wilmington), Martin Tobin (Chicago), Stephen Donohue (New York), John Fisher (Little Rock), Thomas Greylisch (Hartford), Walter Sinnott (Syracuse), Austin Dignam (Hartford), Francis Phelan (Boston)

THIRD ROW: Thomas McKenna (New York), Vincent Hickey (Boston), Thomas Hart (Chicago)

CLASS OF 1919 ►

FRONT ROW: Walter Nott (Richmond), Thomas Harrington (Columbus), Msgr. Bernard Mahoney (Spiritual Director), Gregory Keller (Little Rock), John Salesses (Providence)

SECOND ROW: Francis Mueller (Chicago), Aloysius Ludden (Chicago), Timothy Rowan (Chicago), Thomas Torney (Chicago), John Sprengel (Chicago), Henry Sheiermann (St. Louis), Emmett O'Connor (Albany), Edwin Shaunessy (Richmond)

◄ CLASS OF 1920

FRONT ROW: Thomas MacLaughlin (New York), Thomas Walsh (Brooklyn), Charles A. O'Hern (Rector), John Mahony (Brooklyn), Michael Keyes (Mobile)

SECOND ROW: Eugene Nolan (Brooklyn), David Lynch (Brooklyn), James Smith (Brooklyn), Edward Waldron (Brooklyn), Charles Hynes (Brooklyn)

◄ CLASS OF 1921

LEFT: Michael A. Geehan (San Antonio)

RIGHT: Patrick E. Nolan (St. Augustine), Patrick G. McGill (St. Augustine)

◀ CLASS OF 1922

FRONT ROW: Anthony Gallagher (Toledo), Msgr. Charles A. O'Hern (Rector), Ignatius Kelly (Toledo)

SECOND ROW: John Kane (St. Louis), Leo Burns (Philadelphia), John Fearns (New York), Jeremiah Toomey (New York)

Class of 1923

Photo not available.

CLASS OF 1923 ▶

William V. Donnelly (Albany), Richard J. Gabel (Toledo), Edmund F. Gibbons (Buffalo), James W. Gibbons (Philadelphia), John J. Hartigan (New York), Thomas J. Hayes (New York), Rudolph A. Kraus (New York), Edward G. Raelker (Cincinnati), John Russell (Baltimore), Howard Smith (Cleveland), Joseph A. Tyltheridge (New York)

CLASS OF 1924 ▶

Front Row: John Johnson (Boston), Thomas Hayes (New York), Francis Byrne (Richmond), Carl Hensler (Pittsburgh), Thomas O'Rourke (Brooklyn), Msgr. Charles O'Hearn (Rector), James Collins (Albany), Phillip Matthews (Winona), John Nelligan (New York), Peter Guterl (Newark), Anthony Morrisey (San Francisco)

Second Row: Raymond McQuillan (Erie), Elwood Purick (Brooklyn), Martin O'Connor (Scranton), Leo Pulling (Buffalo), John O'Leary (Boston), Franck Zioltkowski (St. Cloud), Thomas Jones (St. Augustine), William Murray (Brooklyn), Rudolph Kraus (New York), William Reeves (St. Louis), Richard Gabel (Toledo), William Hickey (Trenton), Joseph McFarland (Cincinnati), Joseph Collins (Winona)

Third Row: Edward Roelker (Cincinnati), Leo Binz (Rockford), Jeremiah Davern (Syracuse), Harold Dilger (Newark), James Comerford (Brooklyn), Edward Gaffney (New York), John Kennedy (San Francisco), Gerald Geisen (Covington), Frank Harrington (Helena), William Church (Syracuse)

◀ CLASS OF 1925

Front Row: Luke Owens (Pittsburgh), John Casey (Albany), Frank Johns (Cleveland), John Flynn (Dubuque), Msgr. Eugene Burke (Rector), Leo De Barry (Detroit), Archibald Stitt (Detroit), Francis Murphy (New York), Allen Babcock (Detroit)

Second Row: Joseph Martin (Philadelphia), Thomas Tobin (Portland, OR), Richard McShane (Boston), John Scanlon (San Francisco), Joseph O'Leary (Altoona), John Rowan (Philadelphia), J. Ryan Hughes (Philadelphia), Adrian McShane (Winona), Ovid Chaput (Boston), Abel Caillouet (New Orleans)

Third Row: Maurice Schexnayder (New Orleans), James Hickey (Albany), John Reidy (Albany), Joseph Rojeman (Rockford), Constantine Ver Hoeven (Boise), Wendelin Nold (Dallas), Leroy Cooney (Boston), Joseph Tully (Rockford), Mitchell Cartwright (Baltimore)

◄ CLASS OF 1926

FRONT ROW: Edward Hanrahan (Brooklyn), Leo Smith (Chicago), Leo Ryan (Winona), Harold McKeon (Albany), Henry Burke (Albany), Rev. Joseph Breslin (Vice-Rector), Howard Shepston (San Francisco), Leo Massei (Richmond), Edward Hoover (Chicago), Sidney Metzger (San Antonio), James Hally (Kansas City, KS)

SECOND ROW: Joseph Lubrecht (Covington), Garret Keegan (Boston), Charles Hunter (Natchez), George Flanigan (Nashville), Eugene Lorenz (Dubuque), Michael Bresnahan (St. Louis), Peter Nolan (Brooklyn), Thomas Cullen (Mobile), J. Stanley Hale (Winona), James O'Toole (Toledo), George Donnelly (Ogdensburg), Gilbert Hann (Baltimore)

THIRD ROW: Gregory Cloos (Chicago), Vincent Haks (St. Louis), John Fagan (Brooklyn), Charles Falk (Los Angeles), John Mahoney (New York), Joseph Lux (Chicago), James Hebbeler (Toledo), John McGowan (Brooklyn), Daniel Markhan (Albany), Jules Daigle (Baltimore), James Walsh (San Francisco)

FOURTH ROW: John Walsh (St. Augustine), James Culleton (Fresno), Peter Cameron (Chicago), Emery Scallon (Alexandria), Bernard Lannon (Albany), Lawrence Daly (Chicago), Albert Higgins (Boston)

◄ CLASS OF 1927

FRONT ROW: Edward Waterson (New York), Herman Mielinger (Rockford), John Cullinan (Altoona), Albert Meger (Milwaukee), Msgr. Eugene Burke (Rector), Msgr. Joseph Breslin (Vice-Rector), Joseph Kelly (Albany), Joseph Cunningham (Nashville), William Hunt (Albany), Michael Hyler (Baltimore), Edmund Perrin (Detroit)

SECOND ROW: John Casey (New York), Carl Holsinger (Dallas-Fort Worth), Frank McNelis (Altoona), Edward Kane (Philadelphia), Edward McMenamin (Erie), William Sweeney (Baltimore), Jules Berger (Sioux City), Leo McCormick (Baltimore), Thomas Kelley (Philadelphia), James Fahey (Boston), Joseph Flanagan (New York), Francis Conroy (Philadelphia)

THIRD ROW: Raymond Kearney (Brooklyn), Alphoneus Manley (Scranton), Charles Giblin (New York), Bernard Cremer (Seattle), Albert Duffy (San Francisco), Justin McCarthy (Newark), James Cronin (San Francisco), John Manning (Charleston), John Linn (Baltimore)

FOURTH ROW: George Burke (Wheeling), Thomas Mitchell (Richmond), Gerald Keegan (Scranton), Arthur Blade (Baltimore), Charles White (Altoona), James Fix (Ogdensburg)

CLASS OF 1928 ▶

FRONT ROW: Aloysius Horn (Toledo), Paul Hodapp (Winona), Charles Dee (Syracuse), Arnold Palen (Winona), Floyd Begin (Cleveland), George McLynn (Richmond), Joseph Zyrd (Marquette), Rt. Rev. Msgr. Eugene Burke (Rector), Charles Quest (Nashville), Joseph Kelley (Providence), Francis Fuchs (Brooklyn), Lawrence McHugh (Winona), Ambrose Layne (Winona), Joseph Blake (New York), Philip Larriviere (Detroit)

SECOND ROW: Webster Kenning (Winona), Le Roy Enzler (Dubuque), Edward Schwegler (Buffalo), James O'Brien (Cincinnati), Thomas Sweeney (Baltimore), Raymond O'Flaherty (Los Angeles), William Walsh (Syracuse), Benedict Killacky (Springfield, IL), Robert Weiskirchen (Wheeling), Joseph A. McShane (Winona), William O'Donnell (Cleveland), William Gauche (Cincinnati), Joseph McGucken (Los Angeles), John Costello (Sioux City), James Clancy (Peoria), Joseph Rzetzko (Rockford)

THIRD ROW: Kennion Fulkerson (Galveston), Henry Drouilhet (Galveston), Dennis Barry (San Francisco), John Kiegan (Boston), James McLauglin (Cleveland), Louis Cunney (Boston), Michael Hurley (Manchester), Charles Schulten (New Orleans), Paul Meyer (Baltimore), Robert Ruffing (Toledo), Louis Mendelis (Baltimore), John Buszek (Cleveland), Charles Mahoney (Providence), Joseph Rapkowski (Brooklyn), Andrew McMahon (New York), Edward Shannon (Portland)

CLASS OF 1929 ▶

FRONT ROW: Wilfrid J. Hayden (Louisville), Theodore C. Wagner (Phildelphia), Raymond P. Reali (San Francisco), Harold J. Bolton (Grand Rapids), Rt. Rev. Msgr. Eugene S. Burke, Jr. (Rector), F. Joseph Manns (Baltimore), Thomas P. Kelly (Philadelphia), Leo J. Dreckmann (Louisville), A. Lauren Sattler (Toledo)

SECOND ROW: Daniel McAllister (San Francisco), Matthew E. Clancy (Toledo), William J. Duffy (Newark), James J. McNany (Erie), J. Donald Wagner (Altoona), John J. Kelleghan (St. Augustine), George W. Ahr (Newark), Francis J. Houlahan (Dubuque), Arthur J. Reilly (Albany)

THIRD ROW: Harry P. Mannion (Belleville), Archibald H. Damm (New York), James P. McLaughlin (Cleveland), Edward C. Bailey (Boston), William E. Collins (Boston), Joseph C. Krug (New York), J. Timothy Gannon (Dubuque), John W. Cunningham (Cleveland)

FOURTH ROW: John F. Mullin (Boston), Thomas G. Mulqueen (Albany), Victor J. Dowgiallo (Baltimore), Charles J. Foley (Boston), Maurice A. Olk (Detroit), John J. Maguire (New York)

CLASS OF 1930 ▶

FRONT ROW: Thomas J. Conerty (Brooklyn), J. William Gorman (Winona), William A. Margerum (Trenton), John B. Grellinger (Milwaukee), John J. Carberry (Brooklyn), Rt. Rev. Msgr. Eugene S. Burke, Jr. (Rector), Francis P. McLoone (Brooklyn), Clark B. Hanna (Rochester), Archibald V. McLees (Brooklyn), J. Bernard Kieffer (Louisville), Francis Beykirch (Belleville)

SECOND ROW: Leo R. Smith (Buffalo), Victor J. Reed (Oklahoma), William F. Klasner (Springfield), Joseph P. Mantle (Boston), Jeremiah F. Minihan (Boston), Keith L. Roche (Peoria), James A. Plunkett (Philadelphia), Daniel B. Powell (Philadelphia), Paul J. Potgens (San Antonio), Jeremiah G. MacLaughlin (Brooklyn), Michael J. McCarthy (Natchez), Thomas J. Walsh (Richmond), Joseph H. Boll (Springfield), Anthony J. Dubinskas (Baltimore)

THIRD ROW: Frank Giri (Mobile), Edward W. O'Flaherty (Los Angeles), Joseph S. Tomicek (Scranton), Francis P. Heavren (Hartford), Joseph E. Davy (Winona), Henry H. Grosdidier (Leavenworth), Louis H. Boudreaux (Lafayette), Rayner A. Olk (Detroit), George T. Koen (Galveston)

FOURTH ROW: Joseph H. Brady (Newark), Bernard L. White (Dubuque), J. Philip Johnson (Springfield), J. Kenneth Spurlock (Leavenworth), S. Ernest Wiley (Nashville), William F. Stricker (Baltimore), Marcus A. Valenta (San Antonio)

◀ CLASS OF 1931

FRONT ROW: Patrick J. O'Connor (Sioux Falls), Thomas J. Kelly (Brooklyn), Reginald S. Billinger (Philadelphia), Joseph A. Ward (Philadelphia), Rt. Rev. Moses E. Kiley (Spiritual Director), Rt. Rev. Msgr. Eugene S. Burke, Jr. (Rector), Very Rev. Msgr. Joseph A. Breslin (Vice-Rector), Charles C. Boldrick (Louisville), Joseph C. Beck (Albany), Martin J. Flynn (Brooklyn), Anthony G. Gerst (Louisville)

SECOND ROW: James G. Hennessy (Boston), J. Kelly Reese (Baltimore), Frederick J. Sprenke (St. Louis), Joseph A. Graham (Philadelphia), John J. Daly (Baltimore), Bernard P. Mangan (Winona), Joseph J. Lamb (Providence), Francis E. Suchauck (Philadelphia), Leo P. Vanderwill (Detroit), Edward G. Murray (Boston), Joseph F. McGeough (New York), James B. Nash (New York), J. Patrick Scott (Los Angeles)

THIRD ROW: W. Joyce Russell (Baltimore), Max Satory (Winona), Patrick N. Gallagher (Raleigh), Francis J. Flynn (Detroit), Milton J. King (Providence), Thomas J. McGee (Brooklyn), Oliver J. Bernasconi (Providence), Philip B. Curran (Altoona), Henry W. Sank (Baltimore), George L. Donovan (Nashville), John S. Kelly (Sioux City)

FOURTH ROW: James F. Coffey (Brooklyn), John T. Wieberg (St. Louis), Matthew P. Stapleton (Boston), Philip A. Herrmann (Erie), Benjamin F. Farrell (Wheeling), Charles F. Dolan (Providence), Edward P. Cushnahan (San Francisco), Edward J. Mattimoe (Toledo), Thomas K. Duffy (Nashville)

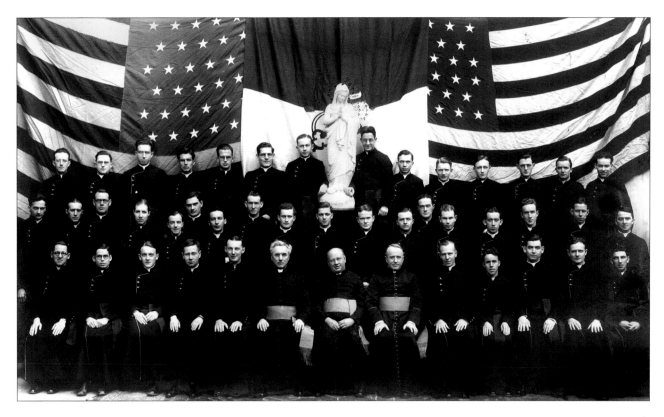

◀ CLASS OF 1932

FRONT ROW: John F. Cody (St. Louis), Lawrence N. Rochon (Detroit), Edward J. La Reau (Albany), Pierre L. de La Ney (St. Louis), Guy B. Hayden (San Francisco), Rt. Rev. Msgr. Moses E. Kiley (Spiritual Director), Rt. Rev. Msgr. Eugene S. Burke, Jr. (Rector), Very Rev. Msgr. Joseph A. Breslin (Vice-Rector), Louis C. Ruth (Raleigh), Joseph T. O'Brien (Albany), Philip A. Farrell (Kansas City), Joseph T. Healey (Rockford), John A. Sears (Boston), William J. Giroux (Scranton), Daniel P. Harnett (Mobile)

SECOND ROW: Joseph G. Gilbride (Scranton), Edward M. Plover (New York), Ronald J. Fannon (Baltimore), Stanley J. Scarff (Baltimore), Albert R. Goetzman (Davenport), Raymond T. Smith (Cleveland), Vincent S. Waters (Richmond), Thomas L. Coonan (Davenport), Francis H. Mendler (Brooklyn), John F. O'Malley (Scranton), William R. Mahaney (Syracuse), John J. Sheeby (Wilmington), Vincent B. Balmat (Cleveland), Maurice J. Tracy (Dubuque), Bernard J. Flanagan (Burlington), William J. Feeney (Boston)

THIRD ROW: James F. Curran (Cleveland), Joseph F. Hale (Winona), William P. Boyd (Scranton), John J. Graham (Hartford), Henry J. Lenahan (New York), Joseph W. Saffer (Louisville), Maurice A. Mullen (Dubuque), Cornelius F. Donohue (Springfield), Joseph F. Connolly (Albany), John T. Murphy (La Crosse), John J. Reilly (Baltimore), Joseph J. Tennant (Brooklyn), Joseph Bracq (Providence), Walter J. Leach (Boston)

CLASS OF 1933 ▶

FRONT ROW: Thomas S. Green (Rockford), Leo F. White (Portland, ME), Clarence A. Batutis (Philadelphia), Joseph M. McCarthy (Philadelphia), Rt. Rev. Msgr. Moses E. Kelly (Spiritual Director), Rt. Rev. Msgr. Eugene S. Burke, Jr. (Rector), Very Rev. Msgr. Joseph A. Breslin (Vice-Rector), John J. Tierney (Newark), Edward J. Craney (Philadelphia), Thomas E. Madden (Altoona), James F. Lafferty (Rockford)

SECOND ROW: F. Harold Noll (Richmond), John F. Sheehan (Helena), James J. Lynch (Spokane), Alfred R. Julien (Boston), Joseph A. Dunn (New York), Michael F. Keehan (Brooklyn), William J. Beane (Providence), Joseph J. Grode (Erie), John J. Heneghan (Brooklyn), Kenneth M. Riser (Richmond), Ronald T. Mentasti (San Francisco), Francis S. Shea (Boston), Lawrence P. Kelly (Albany)

THIRD ROW: John P. Walsh (Scranton), Raymond J. Jansen (Winona), John L. Garvey (Oklahoma), Edward L. Walsh (Providence), J. Leo Linahen (Portland), William K. Dolan (Scranton), Michael K. Carney (Baltimore), G. Carlton Ritchie (Erie), Leonard J. Guzzardo (Rockford), Francis H. Greteman (Sioux City), Nunzio A. Carroira (Boston), Thomas J. Crowley (Baltimore), Stanley Ormsby (Buffalo)

FOURTH ROW: William J. Murphy (Louisville), Leo J. Belanger (Helena), Francis F. Woods (Albany), John A. Suplicki (Buffalo), Charles B. Murphy (Boston), J. Clement Slattery (Providence), Daniel B. Harrington (Helena), John J. Carey (Buffalo), John J. Humensky (Cleveland), Paul L. Richter (Columbus), John J. Cassata (Galveston), J. Leo Anderton (Erie), Clarence J. Yeager (Toledo), John F. Dearden (Cleveland), William F. Kelly (Brooklyn)

FIFTH ROW: Howard M. Merfeld (Dubuque), Paul M. Russell (Louisville), Francis P. Moran (Boston), Henry W. Forester (New York), Louis S. Keller (Covington), Moise R. Gremillion (Alexandria), Philip A. Guarino (Boston), Paul A. McDonough (Manchester), Patrick C. Conway (Sioux Falls), Timothy P. O'Connell (Boston), William J. Sweeney (Trenton)

CLASS OF 1934 ▶

FRONT ROW: Thomas J. McMahon (New York), Andrew B. Deslatte (Galveston), Joseph B. Delahunt (Syracuse), Gerald T. Celentana (Trenton), John J. Dougherty (Newark), Most Rev. Moses E. Kiley (Spiritual Director), Rt. Rev. Eugene S. Burke, Jr. (Rector), Very Rev. Joseph A. Breslin (Vice-Rector), Joseph F. Gannon (Springfield), Anthony J. Ryder (Brooklyn), Joseph B. Brunini (Natchez), J. Joseph Ryan, Jr. (Boston)

SECOND ROW: Alex J. Kraus (San Antonio), James C. McAniff (Rochester), John J. Duggan (Baltimore), Elmer A. McNamara (Rochester), Marcus Murtough (Springfield), John M. Fleming (New York), John C. O'Leary (Altoona), Joseph D. Sweeney (Wilmington), Anthony G. Grutka (Fort Wayne), Stephen Towell (Cleveland), Joseph F. Merluzzo (Providence), Thomas A. Doran (Denver), Robert S. Goshorn (Wheeling), Joseph E. O'Brien (Scranton)

THIRD ROW: Padraic G. Keogh (St. Augustine), John A. Welsh (Nashville), John S. Spence (Baltimore), Walter S. Bush (Nashville), John H. Flanagan (Providence), John L. Morkovsky (San Antonio), Leon O. Englert (Nashville), Joseph S. Ross (St. Louis), Joseph F. Connolly (New York), Donald A. McGowan (Boston)

CLASS OF 1935 ▶

FRONT ROW: J. Edward Goodwin (Cleveland), Robert A. McNulty (Scranton), John A. Donovan (Boston), Christopher J. Gibney (Philadelphia), Henry T. Chapman (Philadelphia), Rev. Charles E. Fitzgerald (Spiritual Director), Rt. Rev. Eugene S. Burke, Jr. (Rector), Rainer De Clerk (Little Rock), William J. Sailer (Philadelphia), Gerald W. Spraker (Baltimore), J. Bernard Moore (Richmond), Richard D. Curtin (Hartford), Charles W. Clifford (Peoria)

SECOND ROW: James T. Shannon (Detroit), C. Bourke Motsett (Peoria), Andrew F. Quinn (New York), Albert J. Hoffmann (Dubuque), William F. King (New York), John T. Feeney (Boston), John F. Mendelis (Baltimore), Frederick Chase (Boston), J. Lennox Federal (Raleigh), Thomas J. Smith (Philadelphia), Francis J. Reilly (Nashville)

THIRD ROW: Dominic G. Scafati (Brooklyn), M. Merwin Lenk (Detroit), George T. Wolz (Columbus), Henry P. Russell (Winona), Joseph J. Carroll (Philadelphia), Avegno L. Souller (Lafayette), Thomas B. Bracken (Sacramento), David P. Collins (Los Angeles), Carl C. Fowlker (St. Louis), James H. Kimberley (Columbus)

NOT PICTURED: John S. Griffey, Jr. (Trenton), John F. Beirne (San Francisco)

Class of 1936

Photo not available.

◀ CLASS OF 1936

Frank Bradican (Richmond), Willis L. Bradley (Rockford), Ralph Broker (St. Paul), James Burke (Belleville), William Chassagne (Monterey-Fresno), William Connor (Omaha), Thomas Coyne (Brooklyn), James Dougherty (Philadelphia), Adrian Dwyer (St. Louis), Louis Flaherty (Richmond), John Fleming (Brooklyn), John J. Healey (Brooklyn), Daniel Honan (Portland), John Horgan (Hartford), Raymond Leng (Milwaukee), David Maloney (Denver), Robert McNamara (Rochester), Michael Melley (Philadelphia), Robert O'Kane (Richmond), Denis Shea (Buffalo), Joseph Shields (Manchester), John Sullivan (Helena), James Weithmann (Erie)

◀ CLASS OF 1937

FRONT ROW: Francis L. Bradican (Richmond), Pasquale L. Ferrara (Davenport), Raymond G. Long (Milwaukee), James S. Dougherty (Philadelphia), James P. Burke (Belleville), Rev. John Cody (Assistant), Most Rev. Ralph L. Hayes (Rector), John A. Reddington (Rochester), Willis L. Bradley (Rockford), Ralph H. Broker (St. Paul), Thomas B. Coyne (Brooklyn), Michael J. Melley (Philadelphia), Christopher E. O'Hara (New York)

SECOND ROW: Joseph E. Shields (Manchester), Gerald F. Millett (Albany), Clarence C. Shoeppner (Santa Fe), William J. Chassagne (Monterey-Fresno), John E. Albert (Baltimore), Daniel J. Honan (Portland, ME), Thomas J. Feeney (Davenport), Carroll T. Dozier (Richmond), Loras T. Lane (Dubuque), Ignatius C. Spenner (Omaha), Charles D. Gorman (Baltimore), John J. Bosa (Manchester), Richard T. O'Connor (St. Paul), Clyde F. Tillman (San Francisco)

THIRD ROW: Michael S. McVerry (Hartford), William P. McMullen (Buffalo), Lawrence J. Malley (St. Paul), David M. Maloney (Denver), J. Louis Flaherty (Richmond), William P. Connor (Omaha), Adrian I. Dwyer (St. Louis), John J. Ansbro (Newark), Thomas P. Scannell (Richmond), George J. Biskup (Dubuque), James W. Weltman (Erie), John M. Curley (Albany), John J. Sullivan (Helena)

FOURTH ROW: James C. Maloney (Louisville), John J. Walsh (Portland), Robert F. McNamara (Rochester), Joseph D. Munier (San Francisco), Robert E. O'Kane (Richmond), Gino J. Monti (Erie), Dennis P. Shea (Buffalo), John J. Fleming (Brooklyn), William J. Bartley (Brooklyn), Kenneth M. Morgan (Brooklyn), John B. Healey (Brooklyn), John A. Horgan (Hartford)

◄ CLASS OF 1938

FRONT ROW: Francis J. Serr (Erie), Edward L. O'Malley (Albany), Walter W. Curtis (Newark), John A. Goodwine (New York), Very Rev. Charles F. Fitzgerald (Spiritual Director), Most Rev. Ralph L. Hayes (Rector), Rev. Allen J. Babcock (Vice-Rector), Thomas F. Little (Brooklyn), George H. Dwyer (Erie), Paul F. Flynn (Albany), Raymond P. Etteldorf (Dubuque)

SECOND ROW: Lawrence J. Ernst (Toledo), Joseph P. Bradley (Baltimore), Peter P. Tuohy (Boston), Richard C. Hiester (Denver), Edward L. Collins (Scranton), Charles G. Maloney (Louisville), Robert L. Arthur (Baltimore), John F. McGlone (Baltimore), Henry G. Beck (Newark), William J. Dempsey (New York), John C. McAlear (Providence), Vincent M. Harris (Galveston)

THIRD ROW: John J. Conway (Syracuse), James J. Hogan (Trenton), Eugene M. Kevane (Sioux City), John J. Quinn (Boise City), John H. Reilly (Hartford), Joseph R. Lacy (Hartford), Cecil E. Finn (Oklahoma), John J. Sheehan (Boston), Russell J. Collins (Boston), Richard K. Burns (Rochester), Anthony H. Deye (Covington), Frederick J. Cardinali (Fort Wayne)

CLASS OF 1939 ►

FRONT ROW: Armand Cyr (Portland), Edward Latimer (Erie), John Connolly (San Francisco), Msgr. Charles E. Fitzgerald (Spiritual Director), Most Rev. Ralph L. Hayes (Rector), Raymond Bosler (Indianapolis), Paul Keeshan (Albany), George Rieffer (Santa Fe), John Pitts (Manchester)

SECOND ROW: Francis Shea (Nashville), Daniel Richardson (Nashville), Edward Seward (Cleveland), Joseph Brokhage (Indianapolis), Edward Catich (Davenport), Emmet Toomey (Davenport), Frederick Freking (Winona), Emmett Murphy (Rochester), Anthony Brouwer (Los Angeles)

THIRD ROW: Peter Schmidt (New York), John Donahoe (Wilmington), Maurice Brauner (New Orleans), William Trower (Los Angeles), James Clarke (Scranton), Robert Goodill (Erie), Robert Walpole (Indianapolis), John Mueller (Green Bay)

CLASS OF 1940 ▶

FRONT ROW: Martin J. Killeen (Camden), Daniel J. Foley (Hartford), Alfred J. Azzo (Duluth), John J. O'Reilly (Wheeling), Very Rev. Allen J. Babcock (Vice-Rector), Most Rev. Ralph L. Hayes (Rector), Josiah G. Chatham (Natchez), Thomas F. Powers (Great Falls), Albert F. Pereira (Richmond), Francis J. Linn (Baltimore), Martin T. Gilligan (Cincinnati)

SECOND ROW: James E. Woulfe (Syracuse), John E. Maney (Rochester), J. Robert Brennan (Savannah), Philip J. Kenney (Manchester), Francis E. Reilly (San Francisco), John J. Kelly (Denver), George M. Spehar (Denver), Philip M. Hannan (Baltimore), Thomas J. Kirk (Philadelphia), Edward J. O'Connor (Camden), Francis B. Kennedy (Cincinnati)

THIRD ROW: James V. Casey (Dubuque), Robert A. Del Russo (Hartford), Maurice J. Dingman (Davenport), Philip F. Lainfelder (La Crosse), Norbert F. Showalter (Dubuque), Paul J. McKensie (Scranton), Bernard D. LaBelle (Detroit), Frank M. Mongeluzzi (Harrisburg), Edward J. Burke (Kansas City), J. Ambrose Devlin (Des Moines)

Class of 1941

Photo not available.

◀ CLASS OF 1941

John Bailey (Baltimore), George Bednartz (Brooklyn), George Brennan (Boise), Francis Carney (Cleveland), Henry Cosgrove (Brooklyn), William Doyle (Baltimore), Michael Driscoll (Springfield, IL), John Duffy (Camden), Joseph Dunleavy (Marquette), Harris Findlay (Richmond), Thomas Greaney (Spokane), James Keogh (St. Augustine), Joseph Labenda (Detroit), Joseph Lehane (Cleveland), Vincent McDevitt (Philadelphia), Francis McHugh (Brooklyn), John Palm (Baltimore), Norbert Richter (Rockford), Lawrence Riley (Boston), Martin Schmitt (Baltimore), Robert Sennott (Boston), Matthew Siedlecki (Harrisburg), David Spelgatti (Marquette), Edwin Stuardi (Mobile), Eugene Sullivan (Philadelphia), James Wathen (Mobile), Aloysius Welsh (Newark), Robert Yates (Toledo), Marvin Young (Detroit)

◀ CLASS OF 1942

FRONT ROW: Joseph McGlinn (Philadelphia), Joseph Breitenbeck (Detroit), Joseph Emmenegger (Milwaukee), Francis Sorci (Buffalo), Marvin McAtee (Owensboro), Most Rev. Ralph L. Hayes (Rector), Joseph Kubik (Detroit), James Leahey (Syracuse), Raymond Eipers (Rockford)

SECOND ROW: Gerald Keiser (St. Louis), John Cain (Newark), John Metz (Harrisburg), Charles Dignam (Los Angeles), Ralph Kowalski (Detroit), Tom Fitzgerald (Lansing), Joseph Spitzig (Cleveland), Robert Anderson (Raleigh), Lawrence Graves (Little Rock), Emmett O'Neil (Helena), George Eagleton (Reno), Charles Collins (Erie), Robert Burrough (Detroit), Thomas Sabrey (Columbus), Michael Murphy (Cleveland)

THIRD ROW: Charles Koester (St. Louis), Robert Hoevel (Fort Wayne), Sylvester Benack (Brooklyn), William Braun (Baltimore), John Daly (Brooklyn), Gerard Broderick (Baltimore), Harry Hynes (Philadelphia), Walter Vetro (Brooklyn), Roy Rihn (San Antonio)

FOURTH ROW: John O'Brien (Newark), George Beck (Galveston), Joseph Egan (Rochester), Fred Duke (Baltimore), Howard Noeker (Lansing), Francis Tyrrell (Brooklyn)

Class of 1943

Photo not available.

◀ CLASS OF 1943

Francis Bisenius (Milwaukee), John Boyle (Monterey-Fresno), Frank Bryce (Hartford), Henry Lappin (Portland, ME), Robert Nealon (Scranton), John Neylon (Buffalo), James O'Donahue (San Diego), John O'Neill (Manchester), Mario Piombini (Brooklyn), Anthony Salemi (Hartford), Alfred Seatagata (Providence), Joseph Zahner (Louisville)

CLASS OF 1944 ▶

FRONT ROW: Joseph Stadler (San Diego), Most Rev. Ralph L. Hayes (Rector), Howard Mulcahy (Albany)

SECOND ROW: Russell Kendall (Galveston), Howard Manny (Albany), Donald Deuel (Scranton), John Donovan (Milwaukee), Albin Kaczmarek (Scranton)

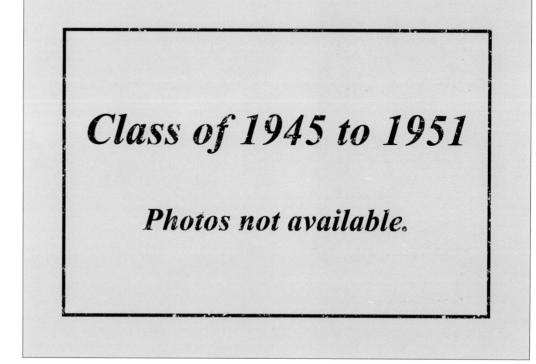

Class of 1945 to 1951

Photos not available.

CLASS OF 1945 TO 1951 ▶

Following the war, the College reopened in the Autumn of 1948 to welcome the future class of 1952.

CLASS OF 1952 ▶

FRONT ROW: Very Rev. Msgr. Richard K. Burns (Vice Rector), Most Rev. Martin J. O'Connor (Rector), Rt. Rev. Msgr. Daniel B. Harrington (Spiritual Director), Very Rev. Robert J. Sennott (Economo)

SECOND ROW: Francis L. O'Hare (Boston), Edward J. McGovern (Providence), Thomas F. Heneghan (New York), Joseph M. Connolly (Baltimore), William N. Holzer (Dubuque), Stanley J. Ott (New Orleans), Charles G. Duffy (Boston), John J. O'Rourke (Providence)

THIRD ROW: Donald B. Zimmermann (Newark), J. Richard Klug (Cincinnati), Daniel R. Callahan (Baltimore), Raymond T. Powers (New York), Robert L. Corbett (St. Louis), James J. Markham (Manchester), D. Philip Dupuis (Lansing), Ronald J. Titus (Galveston)

FOURTH ROW: William J. Petrek (La Crosse), Austin B. Vaughan (New York), Joseph W. Baker (St. Louis), Edward R. Toner (Covington), Joseph L. Battersby (Grand Rapids), Blaine G. Barr (St. Paul), Philip M. Mulcahy (St. Louis)

FIFTH ROW: Charles F. Kordsmeier (Little Rock), J. Clifford Timlin (Scranton), William S. Bevington (Nashville), Richard F. O'Halloran (Boston), Charles P. Essman (Columbus)

◀ CLASS OF 1953

FRONT ROW: Ernest J. Fiedler (Kansas City, MO), Thomas F. Murphy (New York), Very. Rev. Msgr. Richard Burns (Vice Rector), Most Rev. Martin J. O'Connor (Rector), Very Rev. Msgr. Robert J. Sennott (Economo), Robert J. Banks (Boston), Francis A. Galles (Winona)

SECOND ROW: Hilarion V. Cann (Wheeling), Harry Butori (Helena), William Fontinell (Scranton), J. William Houran (Springfield, IL), Joseph W. Hartman (Washington, DC), Richard A. Hughes (Washington, DC)

THIRD ROW: Eugene C. Best (Cleveland), John E. Twomey (Milwaukee), George B. McFadden (Sioux City), Daniel A. Cronin (Boston), James F. Chambers (Buffalo), Richard C. Wempe (Kansas City, KA), Thomas M. Nunan (Mobile)

FOURTH ROW: Alexius Arnoldin (Harrisburg), John Ivers (Philadelphia), Donald E. Sullivan (St. Louis), Maurice C. Dealon (Austin), Harold M. McKennett (Portland, OR), James F. Halpine (Oklahoma City-Tulsa), Paul C. Pelletior (Saginaw)

FIFTH ROW: Donald J. Starkey (Galveston), W. Stanly Fleming (Covington), J. Warron Holleran (San Francisco), David A. Wheeler (Dubuque), Henri I. Foltz (Wilmington), Ralph J. Lawrence (Cincinnati), Charles W. Elmer (Marquette)

◄ CLASS OF 1954

FRONT ROW: John McCabe (New York), Manuel Rodriguez (Santa Fe), John Quinn (San Diego), David Murphy (Rochester), Thomas Duffy (Washington, DC), Edward Cormier (Worcester), Arthur Valade (Detroit), James Cooney (Columbus), John Cotter (Denver), Francis Stangl (St. Louis), Paul Hirtz (Cleveland)

SECOND ROW: Dan Menniti (Harrisburg), Joseph Dillon (Oklahoma City-Tulsa), George Duritsa (Youngstown), Robert Sampon (Milwaukee), George King (Boise), Donald Hellmann (Covington), Stanley Luehrmann (Cincinnati), John Malik (La Crosse), James Boyce (Savannah-Atlanta), Raymond Kevane (Sioux City), John Marshall (Worcester), Donald Kemper (St. Louis)

THIRD ROW: Dominic Bebek (Los Angeles), Edward Keyes (Springfield, MA), Arthur Dernbach (Portland), Robert Willi (Albany), Bernard Gerhardt (Washington, DC), Charles Von Ewu (Boston), William Loftus (Scranton), Roy Literski (Winona), John Weaver (Los Angeles), Joseph Frates (Boston)

NOT PICTURED: Francis Burton (Galveston), Dean Walz (Dubuque)

CLASS OF 1955 ►

TOP ROW: John P. Reilly (Providence), James D. Schumacher (Fargo), Richard A. Maufort (Green Bay), Patrick F. Schoen (Grand Rapids), John D. Thomas (Worcester), Richard E. Zenk (Sioux City), Louis A. Evangelisto (Hartford), John M. Steichen (Oklahoma City-Tulsa)

SECOND ROW: David F. Born (Youngstown), George H. Sallaway (Amarillo), John C. Friedell (Dubuque), Anthony J. Lickteig (Kansas City), Vincent J. Fox (New York), Charles H. Schettler (Oklahoma City-Tulsa), Charles J. Mallet (Lafayette), Vito C. DeCarolis (Hartford), Joseph P. Brennan (Rochester)

THIRD ROW: V. Jerome Walz (St. Louis), J. Patrick Shanahan (Detroit), Joseph P. Casbin (Springfield), Lionel A. Blain (Providence), Joseph L. Byrne (Helena), James J. Doherty (Indianapolis), Sylvester L. Fedewa (Lansing), William J. Forster (Boston), William J. LaDue (Milwaukee)

BOTTOM ROW: Carroll E. Sattersfield (Baltimore), Eugene C. Kane (Cleveland), Harold P. Darcy (Newark), Raymond E. Hamilton (Denver), Most Rev. Martin J. O'Connor, (Rector), Robert F. Trisco (Chicago), Thomas J. Moorman (Salt Lake City), F. Allan Conlan (Scranton), Francis A. Toumier (Santa Fe)

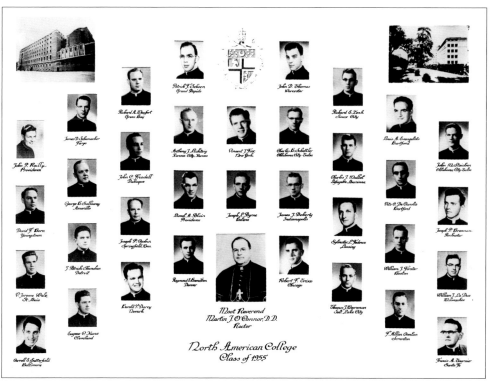

CLASS OF 1956 ▶

Top Row: Rev. Raymond T. Powers (Asst. Vice Rector), Rt. Rev. Msgr. Frederick W. Freking (Spiritual Director), Most Rev. Martin J. O'Connor (Rector), Rt. Rev. Msgr. Francis F. Reh (Vice Rector), Rev. George A. Schlichte (Economo)

Second Row: Luke A. Miranda (Dallas-Ft.Worth), Joseph A. Hartleben (Camden), Harold J. O'Donnell (San Francisco), F. Joseph Gossman (Baltimore), John A. Sullivan (Paterson), Bernard C. Schlegel (Newark), Donald C. McLeaish (Austin)

Third Row: Richard J. Mahowald (Sioux Falls), Edward L. Bode (St. Louis), Thomas E. Wright (Reno), David H. Warren (Owensboro), Daniel E. Kelleher (Denver), Joseph C. Mercier (Natchez), Thomas M. Kelly (Chicago), Patrick J. Gillgannon (Kansas City, MO), William J. Winter (Pittsburgh)

Fourth Row: L. Kevin Conners (Ogdensburg), J. Thomas Finucan (La Crosse), Robert J. Mahoney (St. Joseph), James F. Connelly (Philadelphia), James L. Harrison (Savannah-Atlanta), William G. Ripperger (Indianapolis), John P. Ashton (Youngstown), Virgil F. Gradowski (Saginaw), John F. McCarthy (Helena)

Bottom Row: James W. DeAdder (Boston), William H. Keeler (Harrisburg), J. Paul O'Connor (Youngstown), William J. Cosgrove (Rochester), Clement J. Handren (Albany), James O. Barta (Dubuque), Richard L. Foley (Hartford), John R. Roos (Albany), Eugene L. Gunning (Scranton)

CLASS OF 1957 ▶

Top Row: Armando Annunziato (Fall River), John Baer (San Diego), Edward Bayer (Baltimore), Henry Bowen (Worcester), John Boyle (Davenport), James Brandes (San Antonio), George Brucker (Albany), Gerald Conway (Winona), Thomas Crane (Buffalo)

Second Row: Gerald Curtin (St. Louis), Francis De Domenico (Newark), Philip Dowling (Philadelphia), Charles Eckermann (Syracuse), Philip Farley (Philadelphia), Edward Farrell (Detroit), Frank Foret (Alexandria), Michael Gilleece (New York), Wilfred Gregoire (Providence)

Third Row: Raymond Lessard (Fargo), William Heber (Dubuque), James Heyl (Pittsburgh), Keith Hosey (Lafayette, IN), James Imesch (Detroit), Kevin Kelly (New York), Simon Kelly (Worcester), Charles King (Dallas-Ft Worth), John Koelsch (Boise), Paul Larkin (Washington), Oscar Lipscomb(Mobile-Birmingham)

Fourth Row: Leo Lynch (Saginaw), John McGraw (Syracuse), Robert McKillip (La Crosse), Robert McMahon (Raleigh), John McMurry (Nashville), Daniel Maguire (Philadelphia), Joseph Martin (Boston), Adrian Mercier (Natchez), Howard Metzger (Baltimore), Raphael Michalski (Saginaw), Thomas Lynch (Hartford)

Fifth Row: Edward Mitchell (Fall River), Donald Moeller (Covington), William Moran (Dallas-Ft Worth), Lawrence Murphy (Boston), Joseph O'Brien (Washington), Roderick O'Connor (Raleigh), Robert Plotke (Chicago), John Portman (San Diego), Patrick Quirk (Oklahoma City-Tulsa)

Bottom Row: James Schaefer (Baltimore), David Schilly (Wilmington), Paul Sheridan (Springfield, IL), James Shortal (Springfield, IL), Robert Taylor (Winona), Daniel Tranel (Rockford), Leonard Urban (Denver), John Wakeman (Alexandria), Bernard Zakarezski (Buffalo)

Not Pictured: Claire Maroney (Pittsburgh), Thomas Casper (Louisville)

◄ CLASS OF 1958

FRONT ROW: Martin J. McNulty (Denver), Jesse L. Creel (Raleigh), Rev. John A. Marshall (Asst.Vice-Rector), Msgr. George A. Schlichte (Economo), Msgr. Francis F. Reh (Vice-Rector), Most Rev. Martin J. O'Connor (Rector), Msgr. William A. Bachmann (Spiritual Director), Msgr. Loras J. Waters (Spiritual Director), Rev. Robert F. Williams (Asst. Vice-Rector), James A. Ranieri (Washington), Russell G. Ruffino (Newark)

SECOND ROW: Francis V. Bielski (Philadelphia), Anthony M. Milone (Omaha), Robert E. Hunt (Newark), Alfred C. Hughes (Boston)

THIRD ROW: Thomas P. Johnston (Los Angeles), John F. Morrissey (Worcester), Stephen C. Nevin (Ogdensburg), James K. Crowe (Buffalo), Robert J. Reinke (Covington), James M. Hobein (Marquette), George W. Malzone (Washington), Frederick J. Murphy (Boston)

FOURTH ROW: Francis E. Rett (Boston), Joseph R. Haggerty (Winona), J. Francis Stafford (Baltimore), Lawrence K. Breslin (Cincinnati), Mark J. Schumacher (Green Bay), John A. George (Detroit), Thomas J. Manonski (New York), William G. Mark (Camden)

FIFTH ROW: J. Thomas Moran (Buffalo), John J. Fauser (Detroit), Thomas P. Sosinski (Madison), Andrew L. Nelson (Green Bay), John B. Scorzoni (Boston), William M. Murnion (New York), Edward C. Arnold (Nashville)

SIXTH ROW: Joseph W. James (Amarillo), Joseph P. Higgins (Madison), James W. Moynihan (Rochester), Carl J. Peter (Omaha), Peter P. Silvinskas (Philadelphia), William K. Sheridan (Greensburg), James A. Coriden (Gary)

SEVENTH ROW: Edward M. Egan (Chicago), Roger C. Roensch (Milwaukee), Neil W. Tobin (Dubuque), John P. Graven (Fargo), Gerald P. Boudreaux (New Orleans), Robert H. Bissot (Grand Rapids), Charles J. Zaunbrecher (Lafayette), George O. Lange (Worcester), Timothy Gollob (Dallas-Fort Worth)

◄ CLASS OF 1959

FRONT ROW: Desmond J. Vella (New York), Gaston R. Des Harnais (Detroit), Manuel U. Lucerno (Salt Lake City), Donald P. Brice (Washington), Thomas P. Hadden (Raleigh), James F. Smurl (Scranton), Thaddeus S. Maida (Pittsburgh), Laurence A. Mullins (Davenport)

SECOND ROW: P. Francis Murphy (Baltimore), James Hoelscher (San Antonio), David Jones (Oklahoma City-Tulsa), Vincent Bartolini (Providence), Henry Cody (Hartford), James Flood (Philadelphia), Angelo Caliguiri (Buffalo)

THIRD ROW: Thomas Kramer (Bismark), Joseph Bourgeois (New Orleans), Charles McDonald (Louisville), Herman Lutz (Indianapolis), Andrew Fischer (Portland, OR), Alexander Brunett (Detroit), Francis Friend (Charleston), Antoine Attea (Buffalo)

FOURTH ROW: Joseph McGee (Louisville), Hilary Seubert (LaCrosse), Frank Ruppert (Washington), Anthony Blaufuss (Kansas City), Maurice McCormick (San Francisco), Clement DeWall (Denver), Bernard Roschke (La Crosse)

FIFTH ROW: George John Folster (Fall River), John Rossiter (Kansas City), Donald Durand (Portland, OR), Edward Ciuba (Newark), Vincent Daily (Boston), Leonard Scharmach (Milwaukee), Stephen Slavik (Altoona-Johnstown), Zigford Kriss (Hartford)

SIXTH ROW: John Waldron (Albany), Charles Curran (Rochester), Walter Niebrzydowski (New York), Lawrence Watts (Natchez-Jackson), J. Timothy Leonard (Cincinnati), Francis Moselein (Raleigh), John Keating (Chicago), George Saladna (Pittsburgh), Stanley Schlarman (Belleville), Terrence Monihan (Philadelphia)

CLASS OF 1960

FRONT ROW: Ralph Gillis (Green Bay), William Whalen (Milwaukee), John Poerio (Lafayette), Philip Verhalen (Spokane), Terrell Solana (St. Augustine), Anthony Massimini (Philadelphia), Patrick Cooney (Detroit), David Sorohan (Columbus), Charles Benedetti (Columbus)

SECOND ROW: Philip Zediker (Yakima), Theodore Franck (Richmond), John Lang (St. Louis), Howard Russell (Albany), Vincent Donovan (Washington), Roger Augustine (Sioux City)

THIRD ROW: Valentine Peter (Omaha), James Kastner (Oklahoma City-Tulsa), William Leahy (Philadelphia), James Roache (Chicago), Andrew Schumacher (Boise), Richard Sklba (Milwaukee), John Hotchkin (Chicago)

FOURTH ROW: Thomas Etten (La Crosse), Gerald Flannery (Detroit), John Stewart (Springfield), Donald Hunter (Springfield), John Barker (Louisville), Robert Pusch, (Milwaukee), Wayne Hayes (Monterey-Fresno)

FIFTH ROW: Gerald Sande (Fargo), Joseph Mattern (Fargo), Ralph Platz (Los Angeles), Leo Horrigan (Denver), Richard Jozwiak (Saginaw), Peter Kearney (New York), Anthony Padovano (Newark), John Wayne Hayes (Monterey-Fresno)

SIXTH ROW: Francis Connolly (Raleigh), Francis Weldgen (Buffalo), William Barnett (Camden), Robert Sanchez (Santa Fe), Frank Voellmecke (Cincinnati), William Provosty (Alexandria), Joseph Benger (Corpus Christi), William Mertes (Covington)

SEVENTH ROW: Paul O'Hearn (Boston), William McCarthy (Hartford), Patrick Hazel (Dallas – Fort Worth), Bruce Streett (Little Rock), Henry Kelly (Oklahoma City-Tulsa), Carroll Dupuis (Lafayette), Henry Dougherty (Brooklyn)

CLASS OF 1961 ▶

FRONT ROW: Lester D. Burgmeier (Indianapolis), John E. Flavin (Chicago), Philip A Magaldi (Providence), Thomas S. Maloney (Louisville), LeRoy Seuntjens (Sioux City), Thomas J. McDonnell (Boston), Frederick J. Helduser (Philadelphia), James R. Tracy (Camden), John F. Mahoney (Boston)

SECOND ROW: William J. Marcotte (San Diego), John J. Bagley (Worcester), William C. Hunt (St. Paul), Raymond O. Beauregard (Norwich), Robert D. Lunsford (Lansing), Joseph F. Rebman (Wilmington), Victor B. Galeone (Baltimore), Norman F. Josaitis (Detroit), Peter Zavadowsky (Chicago)

THIRD ROW: Ambrose B. DePaoli (Miami), Gene A. Herbster (Newark), Malcolm J. McLean (Portland), John T. Franklin (Springfield, IL), Lawrence S. Cunningham (St. Augustine), Victor J. DeSantis (Albany), Joseph B. Denning (Davenport), Henry L. Govert (Gary), Thomas J. Sutherland (Detroit)

FOURTH ROW: Walter M. Weerts (Springfield, IL), Russell M. Bleich (Dubuque), Thomas M. McFadden (Brooklyn), Joseph P. Delaney (Fall River), James B. O'Hara (Baltimore), J. David LaTulip (Syracuse), John A. Wall (Raleigh), Edward J. Dillon (Rochester), Charles A. Jackson (Columbus)

FIFTH ROW: Charles R. Dautremont (Grand Rapids), Gerald F. O'Sullivan (Newark), Francis C. Partridge (Grand Rapids), Edward M. Ourada (Omaha), Richard J. DeGrood (Winona), Thomas G. Votraw (Ogdensburg), Samuel B. Wheeler (Albany), Joseph P. Sheehan (Hartford), A. Richmond Gill (Nashville)

SIXTH ROW: John W. Groutt (Pittsburgh), William J. Tobin (New York), R. Allen Hickey (Youngstown), Roy K. Roland (Buffalo), Charles M. Pugh (San Antonio), Paul W. Harting (St. Louis)

NOT PICTURED: Richard C. Breitbach (Milwaukee), Fabian W. Bruskewitz (Milwaukee), Lawrence B. Guillot (Kansas City-St Joseph), John F. Krebs (Pittsburgh), Lawrence M. O'Donnell (Brooklyn)

Class of 1962 ▶

Front Row: Edward W. Kmiec (Trenton), James S. O'Leary (Lansing), James D. McGovern (Camden), Paul Misner (Pittsburgh), Bruce R. Allison (Erie), James W. Flanagan (Dubuque), James B. Joy (Wilmington), Dominic Raspallo (Providence), John C. Favalora (New Orleans)

Second Row: Stephen L. Boemker (La Crosse), Robert S. Flagg (Baltimore), Francis A. Gallagher (Toledo), Frank R. Ferrara (Greensburg), John Vlazny (Chicago), Ernest C. Hepner (Cleveland), James E. Auth (Toledo), Clarence L. Fisher (Camden)

Third Row: Gerald F. Lyons (Trenton), Thomas R. Flynn (Helena), R. Joseph James (Birmingham-Mobile), Anthony A.F. Leuer (Los Angeles), Paul B. Archambault (Portland, ME), Robert F. Rizzo (Albany), Anthony F. Pease (Ogdensburg)

Fourth Row: William J. Hennessey (Miami), Jay R. Dolan (Bridgeport), James M. Mackey (Albany), La Roy Linnebur (Wichita), James J. Mulligan (Allentown)

Fifth Row: John A. Mulryan (New York), Thomas J. Driscoll (Bridgeport), William J. Levada (Los Angeles), James B. Ecarius (Saginaw), Joseph P. Breen (Nashville), Donald F. Smith (Oklahoma City-Tulsa), Richard E. Lutgen (Salina), Donald C. Smith (Newark)

Sixth Row: Ronald F. Whitlow (New Orleans), W. Jerome Sullivan (Buffalo), William J. Hoffman (Atlanta), Charles M. Murphy (Portland, ME), Edward J. Mike (Grand Rapids), R. Thomas Venne (Milwaukee), William L. Gardner (Wheeling), Francis X. Meehan (Philadelphia)

Seventh Row: Charles A. Reilly (Newark), James E. Schott (New Orleans), Donald F. Dunn (Denver), Richard R. Russell (Hartford), James P. Grace (Brooklyn), Robert P. Mahoney (Chicago), Donald C. Grass (Gary), Robert J. Schihl (Buffalo)

Not Pictured: Timothy J. Shea (Boston), Robert C. Densmore (Manchester), Francis J. Beeda (Scranton), John P. Tierney (Louisville), David C. Adams (Lansing), Raymond J. Kelly (Brooklyn), Thomas G. Doran (Rockford), Tod Brown (Monterey-Fresno)

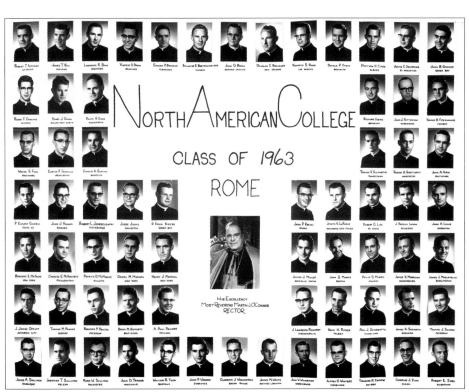

◀ Class of 1963

Top Row: Robert Altmar (La Crosse), James Bill (San Francisco), Lawrence Bock (Hartford), Vincent Breen (Brooklyn), Edward Brennan (Cleveland), Sylvester Bretschneider (Camden), John Brock (Jackson), Douglas Brougher (New Orleans), Kenneth Buhr (Los Angeles), Donald Casey (Brooklyn), Matthew Clark (Albany), Anton Dechering (St. Augustine), John Dewane (Green Bay)

Second Row: Roger Donohue (Winona), Henry Drozd (Dallas-Fort Worth), Ralph Dwan (Washington), Richard Ferris (Brooklyn), John Fetterman (Harrisburg), Thomas Fitzsimmons (Camden)

Third Row: Wayne Funk (Baltimore), Enrico Garzilli (Providence), Charles Giacosa (Nashville), Thomas Gilmartin (Youngstown), Robert Grattarati (Worcester), John Gray (Baltimore)

Fourth Row: Philip Guerin (Santa Fe), John Hazard (Chicago), Roger Jedrzeljewski (Pittsburgh), Jesse Judice (Galveston), R. David Kiefer (Green Bay), John Krejci (Omaha), Joseph La Barge (Oklahoma City-Tulsa), Robert Liss (St. Louis), J. Patrick Logan (Rochester), John Louis (Scranton)

Fifth Row: Bernard McGinn (New York), Charles McGroarty (Philadelphia), Patrick McManus (Duluth), David Madura (New York), Henry Mansell (Burlington), Julian Miller (Rockville Centre), John Morris (Boston), Philip Morris (Newark), James Morrison (Ogdensburg), James Moscatello (Burlington)

Sixth Row: James Offutt (Jefferson City), Thomas Powers (Albany), Bernard Prusax (Paterson), Brian Rafferty (Baltimore), A. Paul Reicher (Chicago), J. Lawrence Richardt (Indianapolis), Kevin Ricker (Toledo), Paul Sciarrotta (Cleveland), James Suchocki (Saginaw), Thomas Suchon (Paterson)

Bottom Row: James Sullivan (Dubuque), Jerome Sullivan (Helena), Mark Sullivan (Rochester), John Trager (Louisville), William Tuyn (Buffalo), John Wagner (Syracuse), Clarence Wagenspack (Baton Rouge), James Watts (Natchez-Jackson), John Wildeman (Harrisburg), Alfred Winters (Cleveland), Theodore Zerwin (Detroit), Charles Zinn (Miami), Robert Zoba (Allentown)

Center: Most Rev. Martin J. O'Connor (Rector)

◀ CLASS OF 1964

TOP ROW: Leo Adams (Corpus Christi), Thomas V. Banick (Scranton), Thomas J. Baurenfeind (Baltimore), John Block (Miami), Ronald Bourgault (Boston), Robert Brom (Winona), Robert Brown (Sioux City), Thomas Buyers (Buffalo), Jerome A. Carosella (St. Augustine), John Carville (Baton Rouge), Francis Colborn (Los Angeles), Peter Conley (Boston)

SECOND ROW: Hugh J. Corrigan (New York), John J. Duffy (New York), Eugene Dyer (Rockville Center), Thomas L. Dzielak (Rochester), Grady J. Estilette (Lafayette), Louis A. Fischer (Salt Lake City), Thomas J. Green (Bridgeport), James A. Greiner (Oklahoma City-Tulsa), Thomas J. Harvey (Pittsburgh), Joseph F. Hayden (Louisville)

THIRD ROW: Clare J. Hendricks (Gary), Douglas J. Hennessey (Peoria), John S. Hooper (Oklahoma City-Tulsa), Howard J. Hubbard (Albany), Stephen S. Infantino (Chicago), Charles A. Kavanagh (New York), Francis D. Kelly (Worcester), Richard F. Keolker (Yakima)

FOURTH ROW: Joseph A. Komonchak (New York), Robert P. Kownacki (San Antonio), Gerald H. Krebs (Erie), Edward R. Lavelle (Harrisburg), Vincent E. Lewellis (Allentown), Richard M. Liddy (Newark), James J. Lock (Kansas City-St. Joseph), Thomas F. Luce (Burlington)

FIFTH ROW: David T. McAndrew (Harrisburg), Peter F. Mullen (Fall River), Joseph F. Nelan (El Paso), Leeward J. Poissant (Ogdensburg), Robert F. Preisinger (Omaha), William E. Puechner (Milwaukee), Miles O'Brien Riley (San Francisco), Russell C. Roetzer (Milwaukee), James H. Royle (Newark), William F. Schneider (Trenton), Dennis F. Sheehan (Boston), James H. Smith (Hartford)

BOTTOM ROW: J. Roy Stiles (Louisville), John J. Strynkowski (Brooklyn), Paul K. Thomas (Baltimore), David W. Tracy (Bridgeport), James W. Varty (Detroit), William A. Varvaro (Brooklyn), William G. Warthling (Buffalo), Richard C. Weaver (Dallas-Ft Worth), George P. Wertin (Fargo), Paul F. Wicker (Denver), Raymond O. Wicklander (Chicago), Robert J. Wisemann (Jefferson City)

CENTER: Most Rev. Martin J. O'Connor (Rector), Right Rev. Msgr. James F. Chambers (Vice Rector)

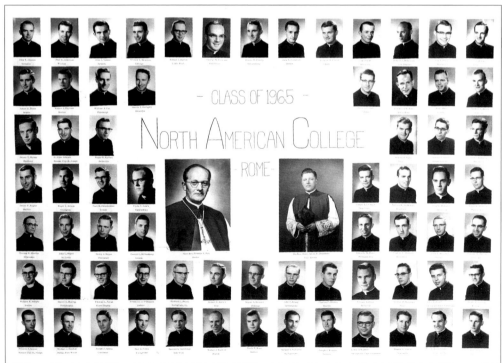

◀ CLASS OF 1965

TOP ROW: John Albosta (Scranton), Paul Alderman (Wichita), John Annese (Newark), Gerald Broccolo (Chicago), Robert Burton (Little Rock), George Coleman (Fall River), Donald Conroy (Greensburg), John Corazzini (Boston), Richard Cronin (Albany), John Cuff (Brooklyn), Robert De La Vega (Los Angeles), John Dillon (Washington), Paul Donnelly (Toledo)

SECOND ROW: James Eblen (Seattle), Walter Edyvean (Boston), William Fay (Pittsburgh), Martin Geraghty (Brooklyn), Peter Gilbert (Albany), Frederick Gunti (Little Rock), Jerry Hardy (Atlanta), Herbert Hauck (St. Louis)

THIRD ROW: James Hickley (Hartford), George Johnson (Kansas City -St.Joseph), Roger Karban (Belleville), Andrea Karg (Erie), Thomas Kelsch (Grand Rapids), John Kinsella (Baltimore)

FOURTH ROW: James Kogler (Buffalo), Roger Kriege (Covington), Paul Kwiatkowski (Toledo), Clyde Lewis (Ogdensburg), Joseph Lynaugh (New York), Patrick McDonnell (Rockford), John McEvilly (Belleville), Robert Manning (Philadelphia)

FIFTH ROW: Thomas Marlier (Milwaukee), John Mayer (St. Louis), Henry Meyer (Cincinnati), Gerald Millenkamp (Omaha), Gregory Moys, (Portland), Charles Mulligan (Rochester), John Mulvihill (Chicago), Anthony Muntone (Allentown)

SIXTH ROW: William Murphy (Boston), Daniel Murray (Philadelphia), Thomas Novak (Grand Rapids), Frederick O'Donnell (Buffalo), Richard Paynic (Springfield), Robert Rarick (Erie), Wayne Ressler (Dubuque), John Rocap (Indianapolis), Charles Rooney (Detroit), William Rowe (Belleville), Michael Ruggaber (Gary), Henry Schlitt (Springfield-Cape Girardeau), Donald Schmitz (Winona)

BOTTOM ROW: Francis Schoen (Kansas City-St. Joseph), Michael Sheehan (Dallas-Ft.Worth), Joseph Speaks (Cincinnati), Paul Tobin (Youngstown), Damian Vallelonga (New York), Walter Waldron (Boston), David West (Detroit), Michael Williams (St. Augustine), Joseph J. Wuybala (Newark), Louis Wyrsch (Springfield-Cape Girardeau), Donald Zanon (Marquette), Joseph Zensen (Los Angeles), John Ziegler (Syracuse)

CENTER: Most Rev. Francis F. Reh (Rector), Right Rev. Msgr. James F. Chambers (Vice-Rector)

CLASS OF 1966 ▶

Top Row: John Ayoob (Pittsburgh), Peter Buchignani (Nashville), William Burke (Chicago), James Buryska (Winona), J. Richard Chachere (Lafayette,LA), Robert Clay (Erie), Victor Clore (Detroit), John Connell (Boston), Daniel Dierschke (San Angelo), Lawrence Dolan (San Diego), John Dorgan (Richmond)

Second Row: David Douglas (Lafayette, IN), H. Tupper Drane (Natchez-Jackson), Robert Faherty (St. Louis), William Freburger (Baltimore), Philip Gallagher (Pittsburgh), Richard Greene (Lafayette, LA), Robert Hickey (New York), Joseph Jacobberger (Portland, OR)

Third Row: Patrick Keefe (St. Augustine), Richard Kelley (Lansing), Donald Klein (Dubuque), James Kossler (Los Angeles), John Lang (Denver), Richard Laveroni (San Francisco), Robert Livingston (Detroit), Joseph Lopez (Amarillo)

Fourth Row: Paul Loverde (Norwich), Joseph McCool (Providence), Michael McDermott (Winona), William Marrin (Rockville Centre), William Marx (Baltimore), Paul Meunier (Wilmington), James Murphy (Albany), William Murphy (Denver)

Fifth Row: James Parker (Portland, OR) James Plagens (San Angelo), Jerome Piotkowski (Sante Fe), Thomas Posatko (Scranton), James Purcell (San Francisco), Lawrence Purcell (San Diego), M. Dennis Putman (Mobile-Birmingham), Edgar Rasch (St. Louis)

Bottom Row: Joseph Reid (St.Paul-Minneapolis), Robert Roh (Lincoln), Joseph Scalzo (Omaha), William Schafer (Chicago), John Schultz (LaCrosse), Anthony Sciotti (Harrisburg), Emil Swiatek (Buffalo), Terry Tekippe (New Orleans), George Thompson (New York), Gerald Vap (Lincoln), Leland White (Charleston), Edward Wieczorek (Youngstown)

Center: Msgr. James F. Chambers (Vice-Rector), Most Rev. Francis F. Reh (Rector)

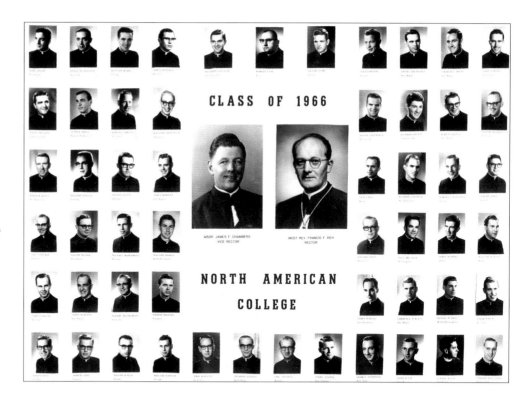

CLASS OF 1967 ▶

Top Row: Paul W. Alandt (Detroit), John A. Alesandro (Rockville Centre), Ronald C. Anderson (Brownsville), David R. Becker (Altoona-Johnstown), Richard A. Behl (Trenton), Joseph C. Benoit (Boston), William F. Berry (Washington), Gerald G. Brennell (St. Louis), Ronald J. Bryda (Cleveland), Charles J. Burkhart (Indianapolis), J. Peter Campbell (Baltimore), Stephen F. Cervoni (Camden)

Second Row: Thomas P. Connor (Philadelphia), James J. Dalton (Chicago), Michael J. Duffy (New Orleans), Dennis E. Dwyer (Denver), Leo J. Feeney (Davenport), George B. Flinn (Altoona-Johnstown), James J. Foley (Philadelphia), William J. Fredelake (Milwaukee)

Third Row: Edward M. Gaffney (San Francisco), Kenneth J. Gallagher (Fargo), Francis T. Goguen (Worcester), Paul M. Goode (Columbus), Charles P. Granstrand (Newark), George M. Griskenas (Chicago), David E. Hauskins (Gary), James W. Healy (New York)

Fourth Row: Anthony J. Keller (Buffalo), Arthur L. Kennedy (Boston), Jerome C. Kern (St Paul-Minneapolis), Dennis D. Klein (Brooklyn), Gerald P. Kobbeman (Rockford), Robert P. La Roche (Manchester), Richard W. Lipka (Wilmington), Thomas F. McDonald (Rochester)

Fifth Row: Thomas McIntyre (Camden), James K. Mallett (Nashville), J. Christopher Maloney (New York), Stephen A. Mandry (Galveston-Houston), M. Stewart Meagher (Pueblo), Joseph J. Merkt (Louisville), LeRoy J. Modenbach (New Orleans), John J. Myers (Peoria), David E. Noone (Albany), Bernard C. Rudegeair (Harrisburg), Dennis W. Raber (La Crosse)

Bottom Row: Joseph M. Novara (Detroit), Michael G. Ryan (Seattle), Charles C. Sebastian (Hartford), Galen M.Scheib (Columbus), John C. Shulte (Saginaw), Lawrence Shelburne (Los Angeles), James J. Schurtleff (Ogdensburgh), C. Gerald Stein (Dodge City), William V. Sullivan (Richmond), Robert L. Theobald (Winona), Frank P. Worts (Camden), Donald W. Wuerl (Pittsburgh)

Center: Msgr. James F. Chambers (Vice-Rector), Most Rev. Francis F. Reh (Rector)

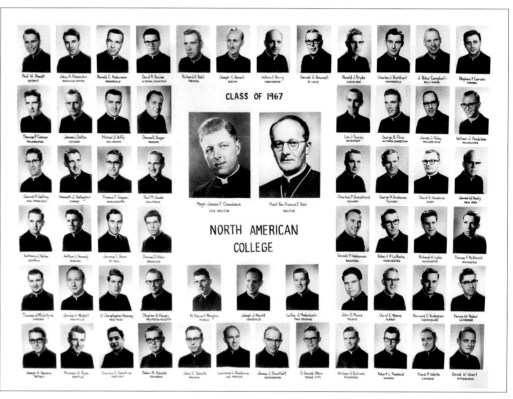

CLASS OF 1968 ▶

TOP ROW – CLOCKWISE STARTING AT 10:00: Donald C. Augustyn (Chicago), John P. Bergstadt (Green Bay), Bernard R. Bonnot (Youngstown), Chester L. Borski (Galveston-Houston), James J. Bretta (Boston), Michael Briggman (Allentown), Kirby G. Brown (Seattle), Charles C. Di Clemente (Wilmington), Peter N. Butler (Ogdensburg), Douglas C. Hoffman (Rochester), Phillip P. Pribonic (Pittsburgh), Jerome F. Weber (Camden), David J. Smith (Helena), Leonard J. Sinatra (Buffalo), Anthony M. Serio (New Orleans), John A. Seck (Kansas City-St. Joseph), Arthur B. Schute (Newark), William R. Schuessler (Rockford), John A. Sandell (Fargo), Paul E. Roder (Sioux City), Robert F. Rank (Green Bay), Paul M. Plevak (Milwaukee), Gerard Dion (Detroit)

SECOND ROW: Richard J. Cassidy (Detroit), Patrick J. Connolly (Gary), John B. Coyle (Toledo), Joseph J. Cuneo (Bridgeport), Francis J. Daly (Boston), Ronald A. Del Ciello (Chicago), Norbert J. Dickman (San Francisco), Jay C. Haskin (Burlington), Richard A. Kramer (San Antonio), M. John Oates (Philadelphia), Ronald V. Nicolosi (Newark), John P. Meier (New York), Andrew E. Martin (Camden), John P. Mahoney (St. Louis), Paul A. Magnano (Seattle), Lawrence J. McGovern (Stockton), Dominic S. Ingemie (Albany), Dennis C. Dorney (Oklahoma-Tulsa)

INNER ROW: Michael A. Joyce (Oakland), Peter J. Drilling (Buffalo), Patrick O. Erwin (Paterson), George F. Ferrick (Los Angeles), J. Joseph Ford (Portland), Gerald Gallagher (Brooklyn), John E. Patrick (Marquette), Albert E. Kirk (Nashville), Robert L. Kincl (Austin), Charles A. Kelly (Richmond), Thomas C. Kelley (Erie), Thomas S. Kane (Rockville Centre)

BOTTOM LEFT: Msgr. James F. Chambers (Vice-Rector)

BOTTOM RIGHT: Most Rev. Francis F. Reh (Rector)

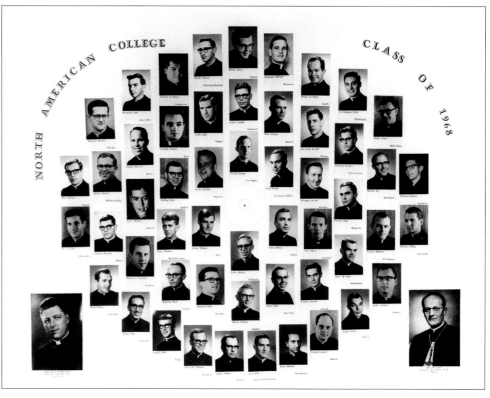

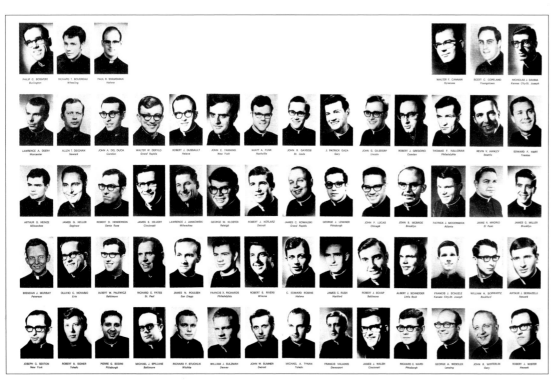

◀ CLASS OF 1969

TOP ROW: Philip Boisvert (Burlington), Richard Boudreau (Wheeling), Paul Bramsman (Helena), Walter Cannan (Syracuse), Scott Copeland (Youngstown), Nicholas Danna (Kansas City-St. Joseph)

SECOND ROW: Lawrence Deery (Worcester), Alan Deigman (Newark), John De Luca (Camden), Walter Derylo (Grand Rapids), Robert Dussault (Helena), John Fanning (New York), Wyatt Funk (Nashville), John Gaydos (St. Louis), Patrick Gaza (Gary), John Gilsdorf (Lincoln), Robert Gregorio (Camden), Thomas Halloran (Philadelphia), Kevin Hanley (Seattle), Edward Hart (Trenton)

THIRD ROW: Arthur Heinze (Milwaukee), James Heller (Saginaw), Robert Henderson (Santa Rosa), James Hilvert (Cincinnati), Lawrence Jankowski (Milwaukee), George Kloster (Raleigh), Robert Kotlarz (Detroit), James Kowalski (Grand Rapids), George Lenker (Pittsburgh), John Lucas (Chicago), John McBridge (Brooklyn), Patrick McCormick (Atlanta), Jaime Madrid (El Paso), James Miller (Brooklyn)

FOURTH ROW: Brendan Murray (Paterson), Olivio Novario (Erie), Albert Palewicz (Baltimore), Richard Pates (St. Paul-Minneapolis), James Poulsen (San Diego), Francis Richards (Philadelphia), Robert Rivers (Winona), Edward Robins (Helena), James Rush (Hartford), Robert Schap (Baltimore), Albert Schneider (Little Rock), Francis Schuele (Kansas City-St. Joseph), William Schwartz (Rockford), Arthur Serratelli (Newark)

BOTTOM ROW: Joseph Sexton (New York), Robert Sidner (Toledo), Pierre Sodini (Pittsburgh), Michael Spillane (Baltimore), Richard Stuchlik (Wichita), William Sulzman (Denver), John Sumner (Detroit), Michael Tynan (Toledo), Francis Valainis (Davenport), James Walsh (Cincinnati), Richard Ward (Pittsburgh), George Wesolek (Lansing), John Winterlin (Gary), Robert Wister (Newark)

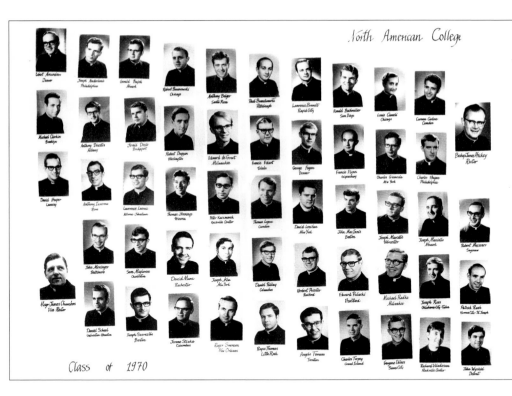

CLASS OF 1970

Top Row: Robert L. Amundsen (Detroit), Joseph J. Anderlonis (Philadelphia), Gerald P. Bajek (Newark), Robert E. Baranowski (Chicago), Anthony J. Bolger (Santa Rosa), Paul J. Brandimarti (Pittsburgh), Lawrence Brandt (Rapid City), Ronald J. Buchmiller (San Diego), Louis J. Cameli (Chicago), Carmen A. Carlone (Camden), Bishop James Hickey (Rector)

Second Row: Michael H. Clerkin (Brooklyn), Anthony C. Diacetis (Albany), Gerald A. Doyle (Bridgeport), Robert D. Duggan (Washington), Edward De Groot (Milwaukee), Francis K. Eckhart (Toledo), George V. Fagan (Denver), Francis J. Flynn (Ogdensburg), Charles R. Giancola (New York), Charles H. Hagan (Philadelphia)

Third Row: David J. Hooper (Lansing), Anthony Insermas (Reno), Lawrence L. Lacovic (Altoona-Johnstown), Thomas J. Jennings (Winona), Peter F. Kaczmarek (Rockville Center), Thomas E. Legere (Camden), David A. Lenihan (New York), John MacInnis (Boston), Joseph A. Marcotte (Worcester), Joseph P. Masiello (Newark), Robert J. Meissner (Saginaw)

Fourth Row: John A. Meninger (Baltimore), Sam R. Migliarese (Charleston), David Mura (Rochester), Joseph P. Nisa (New York), Daniel W. Pallay (Columbus), Herbert D. Priester (Rockfort), Edward C. Pulaski (Hartford), Michael R. Radke (Milwaukee), Joseph R. Ross (Oklahoma City-Tulsa), Patrick J. Rush (Kansas City-St. Joseph)

Bottom Row: Msgr. James Chambers (Vice Rector), Daniel L. Scheel (Galveston-Houston), Joseph F. Scorzello (Boston), Jerome D. Stluka (Columbus), Roger A. Swenson (New Orleans), Royce R. Thomas (Little Rock), Angelo B. Tomaso (Trenton), Charles L. Torpey (Grand Island), Eugene J. Ulses (Sioux City), Richard R. Viladesau (Rockville Centre), John R. Wyskiel (Detroit)

CLASS OF 1971 ▶

Front Row: Francis Virgulak (Bridgeport), George Majha (Manchester), Andrew Golias (Philadelphia), Robert Thelen (Brooklyn), Joseph Martino (Philadelphia), Jerome Krieg (Detroit), Richard O'Connell (Seattle), Thomas Frank (Austin), Gerald Washko (Scranton), Mark Cavagnaro (Camden)

Second Row: Michael Cariglio (Youngstown), Thomas Lehning (Richmond), James Taltavull (Washington), Dennis McCann (Columbus), Cornelius Mahoney (Newark), Richard Marchese (Brooklyn), Walter Cuenin (Boston), Michael Foley (Worcester), Nicholas De Prospero (Pittsburgh), Marcy Rouly (Beaumont), Michael Swalina (Springfield-Cape Girardeau), Robert Sheeran (Newark), Samuel Pilato (Birmingham), Robert Miller (San Diego)

Third Row: Edward Simas (Providence), Albert Reichelt (Baltimore), Michael Servinski (Altoona-Johnstown), Edward Jones (Owensboro), Edward Fitzpatrick (Davenport), John Maksymowicz (Brooklyn), Charles Brambilla (St. Paul-Minneapolis), Michael Johnston (Nashville), Paul Eichhoff (Oklahoma City-Tulsa), Kenneth Steinhauser (Brooklyn), Paul Hinson (Wichita), Charles Przywara (Wilmington), Mortimer Downing (Brooklyn), Peter Donish (Passaic), James Ferruggiaro (Trenton)

Fourth Row: Donn Raabe (Indianapolis), Charles Fanelli (Chicago), James Olsovsky (Galveston-Houston), John Grega (Baltimore), Michael Conley (St. Louis), Edward Holterhoff (Paterson), James Unterreiner (Springfield-Cape Girardeau), Kevin Madigan (New York), Daniel Daley (Burlington), Robert Hayden (Rockville Centre), Richard Roos (Evansville), Kenneth Fischer (Chicago)

Not Pictured: Ernie Marquart (Springfield-Cape Girardeau), Phil Hill (New York)

Class of 1972 ▶

Front Row: Paul E. Coté (Portland, Me.), Michael Fitzpatrick (Omaha), Stanley Ulman (Detroit), Robert Bussen (Salt Lake City), Most Rev. James Hickey (Rector), Rev. Msgr. L. J. Breslin (Vice Rector), John Armistead (Stockton), Jerome Billing (St. Louis), Joseph Keefe (Winona)

Second Row: Michael Mannion (Camden), Stephen Payne (Galveston-Houston), Philip Bloom (Seattle), James Yannarell (Scranton), Joseph Kleppner (Pittsburgh), Thomas Harkins (Camden), Salvatore Matano (Providence), Paul Merry (Bridgeport), V. Paul Fitzmaurice (Greensburg), Robert Bergman (Kansas City, KS), Thomas Kirchberg (Memphis)

Third Row: John Penzenstadler (Green Bay), John Sarge (Saginaw), Edward Kurtyka (Paterson), Richard Rusconi (Paterson), William Karath (Columbus), James Petry (Columbus), Fred Voorhes (Buffalo), Robert Hager (Kansas City-St. Joseph), John L. Sullivan (Pueblo), Robert Sims (Indianapolis), Norman Bauer (Helena), Joseph Donnelly (Hartford)

Fourth Row: Paul Sanchez (Brooklyn), Richard Duncanson (San Diego), Edward Hoffman (Denver), Gregory Holicky (Gary), William Dietsch (Evansville), David Bohr (Scranton)

Not Pictured: Jack Blonski (Gary)

Class of 1973 ▶

William Aaron (Fort Worth), Msgr. William Barry (Pastor-In-Residence), David Baumgartel (Wilmington), John Bida (New York), Rev. Msgr. Lawrence Breslin (Vice Rector), Terrence Brinkman (Galveston-Houston), Laurence Bronkiewicz (Bridgeport), Richard Bucci (Providence), Gary Campbell (Saginaw), William Charbonnneau (Hartford), James Creary (Memphis), Robert Deeley (Boston), Arthur Dennison (Miami), Robert Evans (Providence), Timothy Evans (Pittsburgh), Otto Garcia (Brooklyn), William Glunk (Pittsburgh), H. Martin Hammond (Baltimore), John Heard (Beaumont), Michael Henchal (Portland, Me), Most Rev. James Hickey (Rector), Thomas Leach (Brooklyn), Anthony Litwinski (Detroit), James Ludwikowski (Kansas City, KS), Dennis Malcolm (New York), Vincent Marino (Pittsburgh), Walker Mickless (Denver), John Nienstedt (Detroit), John Murphy (Ogdensburg), Richard Murphy (Baltimore), Thomas Olmsted (Lincoln), Samuel Ritchey (Columbus), Edward Scharfenberger (Brooklyn), Robert Sarno (Brooklyn), David Slubecky (Buffalo), Robert Striegel (Davenport), Thomas Tobin (Pittsburgh), Robert Webb (Raleigh)

◀ CLASS OF 1974

FRONT ROW: John Mancuso (New York), Raymond B. Bastia (Providence), John T. Folchetti (Brooklyn), James McDougal (Lansing), Dennis Ortman (Detroit), Rev. Msgr. John J. McIlhon (Pastor-In-Residence), Bishop James A Hickey (Rector), Msgr. Lawrence K. Breslin (Vice Rector), Timothy M. Mann (Baltimore), F. Terrence Fedigan (Pittsburgh), Joseph M. Matt (Kansas City-St. Joseph)

SECOND ROW: David V. Berberian (Albany), William P. Fay (Boston), Kenneth P. Hallahan (Camden), Dale P. Wunderlich (St. Louis), Mark E. Brennan (Washington), John A. Abruzzese (Boston), David A. Lichter (Milwaukee), Mark A. Svarczkopf (Indianapolis), Eugene T. Gomulka (Altoona-Johnstown), Robert H. Kelly (Altoona-Johnstown), Daniel J. Dillabough (San Diego), Charles Totten (Scranton), Stephen Orr (Des Moines), G. Terrence Steig (Seattle), John P. Vaughan (Owensboro)

THIRD ROW: George A. Stallings (Washington), Joseph W. Bell (Spokane), Gary O. Steeves (Spokane), John S. Schiff (Oklahoma City), Robert A. Byrne (Saginaw), Edward J. Hinds (Patterson), Dennis M Schnurr (Sioux City), John W. Steiner (La Crosse), Donald E. King (Youngstown), Valentine N. Handwerker (Memphis), David P. Hester (Baltimore), Allen H. Vigneron (Detroit)

◀ CLASS OF 1975

FRONT ROW: Dominic P. Irace (Arlington), Michael P. Burnert (Cincinnati), Ronald F. Fishbeck (Galveston-Houston), James M. Farrell (Indianapolis), Peter P. Kenny (Bridgeport), Br. Randal Riede, C.F.X. (Librarian), Rev. Msgr. Harold P. Darcy (Rector), Rev. Charles A. Kelly (Vice Rector), Rev. Vincent J. O'Connor (Pastor-in-Residence), Charles F. Monroe (Worcester), George C. Gustafson (Marquette), William P. Burke (Memphis), Jay T. Maddock (Fall River), Michael T. Donohue (Norwich)

SECOND ROW: Blase J. Cupich (Omaha), Robert J. Gilday (Indianapolis), Dennis M. Hand (Gary), Patrick J. Zurek (Austin), Michael J. Hoeppner (Winona), Michael R. Cote (Portland, ME), David M. Ross (Toledo), Jerome T. Jecewiz (Brooklyn), W. Michael Mulvey (Austin), Martin H. Demek (Baltimore), William A. Ogrodowski (Pittsburgh), David D. Kagan (Rockford), Gennaro P. Avvento (Brooklyn), John F. Kurzak (Sioux City), John J. Mericantante (Boston), W. Jerry Riney (Owensboro), Gregory L. Esty (Minneapolis-St. Paul)

THIRD ROW: Kevin T. McMahon (Wilmington), Raymond L. Burke (La Crosse), Leonard P. Blair (Detroit), Michael F. Simonini (Rockford), Timothy J. Place (Fall River), Ramon I. Aymerich (Buffalo), David H. Carey (Pittsburgh), John R. Smith (Seattle), J. Stefan Pirtle (Owensboro), John P. Gatzak (Hartford), John D. Hortum (Arlington), Daniel L. Williams (Fort Worth), James A. Harvey (Milwaukee), Joseph T. Campo (New York)

NOT PICTURED: Glenn J. Provost (Lafayette)

◄ CLASS OF 1976

FRONT ROW: G. Warren Wall (Mobile), Rev. Charles A. Kelly (Vice Rector), Rev. Msgr. Harold P. Darcy (Rector), Rev. Msgr. Thomas M. Duffy (Pastor-in-Residence), Rev. Msgr. John Tracy Ellis (Scholar-in-Residence), Douglas K. Clark (Savannah)

SECOND ROW: Michael F. Koss (Detroit), James F. Kauffmann (Richmond), Raymond J. Ferrick (Providence)

THIRD ROW: Bernard F. Ronan (Phoenix), Robert G. Lorenzo (Newark), John J. Prendergast (Peoria), Leon F. Strieder (Austin), John P. Zenz (Detroit), Timothy J. Moran (Boston)

FOURTH ROW: Dwayne J. Thomas (Dubuque), D. Terrence Morgan (St. Augustine), Daniel N. Di Nardo (Pittsburgh), John J. Hillenbrand (Stockton), Dennis M. Boudreau (Providence), Eugene E. Costa (Springfield, IL), Michael W. Coe (Evansville)

FIFTH ROW: Timothy L. Doherty (Rockford), Charles D. Balvo (New York), John D. Faris (St. Maron of Detroit)

SIXTH ROW: Mark A. Ressler (Dubuque), C. Christopher Peck (Albany), Rocco C. Memolo (Manchester), William J. Parham (Memphis), Robert J. Wondolowski (Worcester), Douglas A. LaRocca (San Francisco)

SEVENTH ROW: Robert J. Busher (Davenport), Thomas R. DeKay (Arlington), Timothy M. Dolan (St. Louis), Michael J. McKay (San Diego), Charles O. Rouse (Baltimore), Dennis J. O'Connell (Charleston), Bernard E. Yarrish (Scranton), Thomas E. Gullickson (Sioux Falls)

CLASS OF 1977 ►

FRONT ROW: Dennis L. Mikulanis (San Diego), Kevin P. O'Neill (Scranton), Harold J. Buse (Omaha), René T. Mathieu (Portland), Rev. Charles A. Kelly (Vice-Rector), Rev. Msgr. Harold P. Darcy (Rector), Rev. Msgr. Joseph M. Champlin (Pastor-in-residence), James R. Murphy (St.Paul-Minneapolis), Richard A. Marzheuser (Cincinnati), Douglas J. Siebenaler (Toledo)

SECOND ROW: Chester P. Snyder (Harrisburg), Thomas J. Coenen (Des Moines), Mallory M. Thompson (Washington), Earl A. Boyea (Detroit), Paul M. Bomba (Worcester), Antony P. Brescia (Hartford), Stephen M. Di Giovanni (Bridgeport), Michael S. Driscoll (Helena), Jefferson J. De Blanc (Lafayette), Patrick S. Brennan (Portland), David A. Rogerson (Seattle), Peter A. Routhier (Burlington), John M. Baker (Columbus)

THIRD ROW: Edward C. Petty (Dubuque), Alfred H. Fish (Ogdensburg), Michael J. Martinez (Phoenix), Dennis J. O'Brien (Worcester), Christopher J. Schreck (Savannah), Robert J. Oliveira (Fall River), Dale R. Rupert (Scranton), Thomas J. Tiezzi (Hartford), Richard W. Shoda (Wheeling), Charles C. Sauer (Memphis), Michael A. Schoenhofer (Toledo), Barry M. Meehan (Providence), James M. Tranel (Rockford), Peter I. Vaccari (Brooklyn), Michael L. Sturn (San Diego), Danny L. Oswald (Sioux City), John P. Klein (Lansing), James A. Vanderberg (Pueblo)

INSERT: Timothy P. Broglio (Cleveland)

CLASS OF 1978 (PART I) ▶

FRONT ROW: Richard A. Emerson (Gary), Patrick D. Clementz (Rockford), Rev. Charles A. Kelly (Vice Rector), Rev. Msgr. Harold P. Darcy (Rector), Rev. Robert L. Noon (Pastor-in-Residence), Br. Randal Riede C.F.X. (Librarian), Richard M. Colletti (Winona), Brian A. Mee (Spokane), Mark E. J. Nolting (Oakland)

SECOND ROW: Jon-Paul Gallant (Fall River), Normand G. Grenier (Fall River), David R. Perkins (Nashville), Daniel F. Krettek (Des Moines), Kenneth J. Liona (Brooklyn), Andrew J. Lukach (Scranton), Robert T. Sullivan (Boston), Antonio J. Marfori (St. Cloud), Michael C. Stubbs (Kansas City), Joseph L. Tagg (Memphis), John J. Murphy (Camden)

◀ CLASS OF 1978 (PART II)

FRONT ROW: Joseph F. Barr (Baltimore), Ronald L. Bratt (Dallas), Michael J. Culkin (Washington), Patrick J. Dolan (Louisville), Carl D. Recker (Toledo), J. Patrick Manning (Youngstown), Edward P. O'Halloran (New York), J. Peter Sartain (Memphis), James B. Anderson (Galveston-Houston), George G. Matejka (Cleveland), David J. Sanders (Milwaukee)

SECOND ROW: Jay H. Peterson (Great Falls), Steven D. Otellini (San Francisco), J. Scott Duarte (Richmond), Fernando Ramirez (San Diego), Christopher P. Daigle (Tulsa), John A. Prinelli (Richmond), John L. Parr (La Crosse), Mark J. Simeroth (Fort Worth), John A. Hennessy (Fort Worth), Richard W. Walling (Cincinnati), Norman P. Bolduc (Manchester), Charles T. Diedrick (Cleveland)

◂ CLASS OF 1979

FRONT ROW: Francis X. Blood, Jr. (St. Louis), James C. Sheehan (New York), Fay W. Ager (Ogdensburg), Joseph S. Marino (Birmingham), Thomas J. Allsopp (Seattle), Br. Randal Riede, C.F.X. (Librarian), Rev. Msgr. Harold P. Darcy (Rector), Rev. Charles A. Kelly (Vice Rector), Rev. James A. Suchocki (Pastor-in-Residence), Francis C. Santilli (Providence), Edward A. Hankiewicz (Grand Rapids), Patrick M. Jones (Jackson), Robert W. Finn (St. Louis)

SECOND ROW: Warren J. Savage (Springfield, MA), James G. Hannan (Brooklyn), Michael J. Hartwig (Dallas), Daniel J. Kampschneider (Omaha), Kenneth W. Roeltgen (Washington), John A. Renken (Springfield, IL), Gilbert M. Piette (Brownsville), Daniel R. Pater (Cincinnati), Gregory L. Sullivan (Portland, OR), Jeremiah N. Murasso (Hartford), Anthony J. Herold (Davenport), Robert J. Jasany (Cleveland), Donald E. Blumenfeld (Newark), David L. Poulson (Erie), Stephen J. Stavoy (Scranton), John E. Norman (Salt Lake City), John G. Durbin (Altoona-Johnstown), Robert J. Dwyer (Boston), Michael R. Moynihan (Bridgeport)

◂ CLASS OF 1980 (PART I)

FRONT ROW: William Millea (Bridgeport), Miles Walsh (Baton Rouge), James Moroney (Worcester), Bruce Lawler (Sioux City), Anthony Taylor (Oklahoma City), Richard Tomasone (Erie)

SECOND ROW: Joseph Lehman (Richmond), Mark Mazza (Gary), Charles Stoetzel (La Crosse), David Schwartze (Kansas City-St. Joseph), Robert Norris (New York), Keith Vincent (Lafayette), Paul Robicheaux (Alexandria-Shreveport)

NOT PICTURED: Joseph Calise (Brooklyn)

CLASS OF 1980 (PART II) ▶

FRONT ROW: Joseph Busch (Albany), Nicholas Gengaro (Newark), Timothy Clark (Seattle), Rev. Msgr. Charles Murphy (Rector), Rev. Thomas V. Banick (Vice Rector), Justin Langille (San Diego), David Dettmer (Brooklyn), Lloyd Stephenson (Richmond)

SECOND ROW: Robert Everard (Kansas City, KS), Robert Coerver (Dallas), David Drewelow (Springfield-Cape Girardeau), J. Jay Jackson (Memphis), Robert Deahl (Milwaukee), Timothy Boeglin (Fort Worth), John Gallagher (Davenport), Robert Dempsey (Chicago), Robert Alcamo (Newark), Francis Le Blanc (Boston), Christopher Armstrong (Cincinnati), Charles Burton (Nashville)

CLASS OF 1981 ▶

FRONT ROW: Larry J. Kirby (Baker), Stephen G. Gibson (Gary), David F. Hulshof (Springfield-Cape Girardeau), David W. Williams (Hartford), Rev. Thomas V. Banick (Vice Rector), Rev. Msgr. Charles M. Murphy (Rector), Br. Randal Riede, C.F.X. (Librarian), Daniel F. Kassis (Gallup), Stephen J. Avila (Fall River), Stephen J. Binz (Little Rock), John W. O'Brien (Providence)

SECOND ROW: Alfredo Olivas (El Paso), Mark F. Goldasich (Kansas City), George M. Garner (Washington), Kevin C. McCoy (Sioux City), Thomas R. Kopfensteiner (St. Louis), Paul A. Holmes (Newark), David R. Kukielski (Atlanta), Kevin J. O'Brien (Ogdensburg), Gregory R. Hite (Toledo), George E. Baker (New York), Michael J. Curran (Brooklyn), John V. Duhoski (Gaylord)

THIRD ROW: Bruce J. Orsborn (San Diego), Eugene S. Morris (Washington), Robert E. Zapfel (Buffalo), Thomas E. Mischler (Gary), Joseph A. Morgan (Ogdensburg), Nicholas Zukowski (Detroit), Kevin J. Mahoney (St. Louis), Richard J. Gabuzda (Scranton), Robert J. Kropack (Cleveland), Alfred F. Pecaric (Bridgeport), Stephen R. Vellenga (Cleveland), David A. Wolfer (Cincinnati), Michael C. Fedewa (Grand Rapids)

CLASS OF 1982 ▶

FRONT ROW: John Hilton (Denver), Sean McDonagh (Springfield), Norman Nawrocki (Detroit), Francis Hund (Kansas City, KS), Darr Schoenhofen (Syracuse), Rev. Msgr. Charles M. Murphy (Rector), Rev. Thomas V. Banick (Vice Rector), Richard Siepka (Buffalo), David Pietropaoli (Baltimore), Timothy Reker (Winona), Timothy Thomson (Fort Worth)

SECOND ROW: Thomas Loya (Parma), Ben Marcantonio (San Diego), Brent Baum (Baton Rouge), Edward Buelt (Denver), Paul Makarewicz (St. Louis), Daniel Keller (Omaha), Salvatore Cordileone (San Diego), Salvatore Manganello (Buffalo), Robert Cormier (Newark), Robert Flock (La Crosse), Michael Kauders (Baltimore), Gorden Polenz (Albany), Gregory Mansour (St. Maron), Jan Majernik (Gary), Richard Futie (Bridgeport)

THIRD ROW: Dennis Kristof (Parma), Martin Zlatic (St. Louis), William Ford (Stockton), Joseph Tyrell (New York), Joseph Hoppa (Winona), Michael Parisi (Paterson), Edward Smith (Cincinnati), Randy Cuevas (Baton Rouge), Carl Duman (Portland), Michael Thomas (St. Maron of Detroit), Jean-Pierre Ruiz (Brooklyn)

◀ CLASS OF 1983

FRONT ROW: Jeffrey A. Zwack (Bismark), Peter J. Hosak (Eparchy of Passaic), Michael F. Murphy (San Diego), John J. Brown (Brooklyn), Frank H. Rossi (Galveston-Houston), Jeffery A. Largent (Fort Wayne-South Bend), Rev. Thomas V. Banick (Vice Rector), Rev. Msgr. Charles M. Murphy (Rector), Phillip M. Cioppa (Albany), Randall J. Laplante (Worcester), Peter J. Jugis (Charlotte), Vincent J. Dufresne (Baton Rouge), Daniel T. Dupree (Memphis)

SECOND ROW: Carl J. Scheble (St. Louis), Kennon Y. Ducré (El Paso), Leo J. McKernan (Scranton), Randall R. Phillips (Detroit), Bennett J. Voorhies (Lafayette), Kevin C. Rhodes (Harrisburg), Vincent P. Redder (Fort Worth), Richard F. Delaney (St. Louis), John P. McGinty (Boston), Patrick A. Ratigan (Ogdensburg), F. William Etheridge (Rockford), C. Lawrence Miller (Cleveland), Donald W. Hanson (San Angelo), Michael J. Mescher (Dubuque), William B. Neuhaus (Covington), James W. Koons (Fort Wayne-South Bend)

THIRD ROW: Douglas Tufaro (Bridgeport), Joseph C. Gatto (Buffalo), Dale J. Korogi (St. Paul and Minneapolis), Cleo J. Milano (Baton Rouge), David J. Malloy (Milwaukee), Kevin Laugherty (Springfield, IL), John S. Custer (Eparchy of Passaic), Dave R. Ireland (Cleveland), Kenneth M. Del Priore (San Diego), Michael L. Maginot (Gary), John Y. Baltz (Little Rock)

CLASS OF 1984

FRONT ROW: Allen R. Kuss (Bismarck), Terrance W. Klein (Dodge City), Joseph F. Mazurkiewicz (Altoona-Johnstown), Lee J. de Lisle (Norwich), James M. Zaleta (Passaic), Thomas V. Banick (Vice Rector), Rev. Msgr. Charles M. Murphy (Rector), Brian J. McNamara (Rockville Centre), Joseph G. Hanefeldt (Omaha), Joe S. Vasquez (San Angelo), Robert A. Kerr (St. Augustine), James M. Dunfee (Steubenville), Than N. Vu (Baton Rouge), Robert L. Grant (Des Moines)

SECOND ROW: Alexander H. Bradshaw (Rochester), Howard J. Venette (Ogdensburg), James A. Schillinger (Atlanta), John F. Madden (Worcester), James P. McDonough (Pittsburgh), Daniel P. Dower (Worcester), Douglas O. Walthier (Dubuque), Joseph Deichert (Bismarck), Richard E. Donohoe (Birmingham), James J.M. Reynolds (Brooklyn), Kevin S. Cameron (Des Moines), Douglas V. Borowski (Boston), Gregory G. Hart (Little Rock)

THIRD ROW: Steven L. Leger (Beaumont), Marcel Pincince (Providence), William R. Trainor (Worcester), Eddie E. L. Tolentino (Washington), Edmund J. Whalen (New York), Mark R. Schumacher (Boise), Carlos D. Valencia (Brooklyn), Stanley G. Kacprzak (Rochester), Daniel J. Trapp (Detroit), Vincent M. Donnelly (Paterson), David H. O'Connor (Cleveland), John J. McCarthy (Hartford), David A. Fisher (Columbus)

CLASS OF 1985 ▶

FRONT ROW: John Aiello (Memphis), Mark Alise (Baton Rouge), William Bagnola (Youngstown), Msgr. Lawrence Purcell (Rector), Rev. Thomas V. Banick (Vice Rector), Greg Banazak (Detroit), Thomas De Lucci (New York), Stephen Dublinski (Spokane), Joseph Gazarkiewicz (Gary)

SECOND ROW: Timothy Hayes (Columbus), David Hemann (Sioux City), Thomas Murphy (Indianapolis), Thomas Pettei (Brooklyn), Joseph Quinn (Scranton), Robert Reed (Boston), Christopher Repp (Miami), John Riley (Stockton), Kevin Royal (Bridgeport), John Sauer (Winona), Bradley Sterrett (Salina), Kris Stubna (Pittsburgh), Walter Tappe (Washington), Peter Vaghi (Washington), Timothy Vaverek (Austin), Dennis Veltri (Erie)

CLASS OF 1986 ▶

Front Row: Joseph Maddalena (Greensburg), Daniel Flynn (Hartford), Henry Rodriguez (San Diego), William Vouk (St. Cloud), Msgr. Lawrence Purcell (Rector), Fr. Joseph Donnelly (Vice Rector), Thomas Whitman (Erie), Peter Daly (Washington), Michael Gibson (Gary), Kevin McBrien (Brooklyn), Albert Grasher (Spokane)

Second Row: James Meade (Gary), Matthew Huber (Helena), David Li Puma (Buffalo), Michael Schlut (Denver), Michael Sis (Austin), Henry Grantges (St. Petersburg), Patrick McGovern (Brooklyn), James Logan (Baker), David O'Connor (Dubuque), Daniel Murray (Winona), James LeCluyse (Kansas City), Thomas Rozman (Harrisburg), James Geraghty (New York), Christopher Ruhlman (Kansas City)

Not Pictured: Neil Roy (Peterborough)

CLASS OF 1987 ▶

Front Row: Joseph Barbieri (Toronto), Gregory Gordon (Reno-Las Vegas), Joseph Giandurco (New York), Rev. Msgr. Lawrence Purcell (Rector), Fr. Joseph Donnelly (Vice Rector), Joseph Wolf (Buffalo), Andrew Wisdom (Rockford), Christopher Johnson (Worcester)

Second Row: Stephen Vileo (Detroit), Thomas Knoblach (St. Cloud), Anthony Cincinnati (Wheeling-Charleston), Robert Congdon (Boston), James Nadeau (Portland, OR), David Kersten (Buffalo), James Oberle (Washington), Marion Makarewicz (Jefferson City), John Dakes (Washington), David Corley (Tulsa), Kevin Donovan (Hartford), Jack Fondacaro (Brooklyn)

Third Row: Cyril Flavin (San Diego), William Becker (Winona), Joseph Waters (St. Petersburg), Michael Maslowsky (Portland, OR), James Connell (Milwaukee), James Bissonette (Duluth), David Leibham (Austin), Mark Nemetz (Sacramento), David Lobato (Pueblo), Matthew Smith (Providence)

◄ CLASS OF 1988

FRONT ROW: Kenton Sailstad (Duluth), Joseph Kutch (Scranton), Roger Di Buo (Wilmington), Peter Muha (Gary), Rev. Msgr. Lawrence Purcell (Rector), David Schena (Gary), David Bonnar (Pittsburgh), David Buckles (Lafayette, IN), Robert Meyer (Newark)

SECOND ROW: James Watkins (Washington), Michael Lynch (Brooklyn), Stephen Clovis (Portland), Dean Martin (Baton Rouge), Mark Buckley (Peterborough), John Fell (Metuchen), William Aitcheson (Reno-Las Vegas), Frank Dewane (Green Bay), Dean Wilhelm (Austin), Steven O'Hala (Miami), Thomas Euteneuer (Palm Beach), Robert Collins (Brooklyn)

THIRD ROW: Phillip Lavery (Pittsburgh), Michael Banach (Worcester), Mark Mallak (New Ulm), Joseph Siegel (Joliet), William Kelly (Boston), Daniel Mahan (Indianapolis), John Gordon (Newark), Paul de Ladurantaye (Arlington), Christopher Hellstrom (Denver), Gerald Cadieres (Maracaibo), Kerry Sopoci (Duluth), John Eckhard (St. Louis)

NOT PICTURED: G. William Finch (Washington), Mark Wagner (Stockton)

◄ CLASS OF 1989

FRONT ROW: Daniel Mueggenborg (Tulsa), Patrick Smith (Washington), Msgr. Lawrence Purcell (Rector), Rev. Joseph Donnelly (Vice Rector), Paul Leonard (Scranton), Michael Welch (Washington)

SECOND ROW: Michael Huggins (San Diego), Juan Moreno (San Diego), Michael Mulhall (Peterborough), David Herrera (San Angelo), Mark Hammond (Columbus), Heberto Diaz (Brownsville), Ronny Jenkins (Austin), James Torquato (Pittsburgh), Eric Fowlkes (Nashville), Rory Conley (Washington), Thomas Mlodzik (Milwaukee)

THIRD ROW: Charles Christen (Pittsburgh), J. Mark Williams (Peoria), Bernard Hebda (Pittsburgh), William McDonald (Stockton), Robert Hughes (Camden), Joseph Rosie (Trenton), Kevin Louis (La Crosse), Michael Harris (Scranton), Douglas Milewski (Newark), D. Stephen McCrate (Beaumont), Michael Sweeney (Dubuque), John Costello (Brooklyn), Dennis Schmitz (Kansas City), Michael Russo (Lafayette), John Guthrie (Bismarck)

NOT PICTURED: Gerald Rush (Omaha)

◄ CLASS OF 1990

FRONT ROW: Lance Gilbert (Erie), Rev. Msgr. Edwin F. O'Brien (Rector), Kenneth J. Pino (Sante Fe), Kevin P. Riley (St. Petersburg), H. E. Joseph Cardinal Bernardin (Chicago), J. Stephen Vallelonga (Wheeling-Charleston), Rev. Msgr. Stephen Orr (Vice Rector), James Bird (Erie)

SECOND ROW: Charles P. Connor (Scranton), Peter M. McGuine (San Diego), Michael G. Glenn (Denver), Eric S. Powell (Peoria), Michael J. Cobb (San Bernardino), Mark W. Ervin (Washington), Gerald P. Melchior (Omaha), Lawrence M. Lott (Mobile), David J. Lesniak (Detroit), Timothy M. McCarragher (Youngstown)

THIRD ROW: Eric G. Russ (Evansville), Paul J. Thurmes (St. Paul-Minneapolis), Robert F. McKeon (New York), G. Michael Bugarin (Detroit), Joseph H. Metzger, III (Richmond), Peter B. Mangum, II (Shreveport), James J. Midgley (Bridgeport), Michael F. X. Hinkley (Hartford), Jules M. Arceneaux, II (Lafayette), John H. Barkemeyer (Chicago), David P. Fleming (Des Moines), Thien Chi Nguyen, Timothy M. McCarragher (Youngstown), Terence J. Moran (Boston), Thomas P. Voorhies (Lafayette), Stephen M. Staff (Mobile)

CLASS OF 1991 ►

FRONT ROW: Matthew D. Spahr (San Diego), Patrick G. Jerome (Kansas City), D. Gregory Smith (Helena), Rev. Msgr. Edwin F. O'Brien (Rector), Rev. Msgr. Stephen Orr (Vice-Rector), Peter B. Wells (Tulsa)

SECOND ROW: Thomas J. Buffer (Columbus), Brian J. Welding (Pittsburgh), Douglas H. Sousa (Fall River), David W. Cramer (Scranton), Heinrich J. Losemann (Baltimore), Scott E. Bullock (Dubuque), William C. Whalen (Hartford), Everett Pearson (Washington), Paul B. O'Brien (Boston), William F. Fields (Mobile), John R. Gerritts (Superior), Felix Kalinowski (Detroit), John F. Doerfler (Green Bay), Joseph S. Wadas (Mobile), W. Thomas Long (Green Bay), David J. Tokarz (Mobile), John S. Bonnici (New York), C. Gregory Butta (Washington), Michael P. Hermes (Kansas City), Martin R. Schaub (Gaylord)

NOT PICTURED: Joseph R. Reilly (Newark)

CLASS OF 1992 ▶

Front Row: Charles V. Antonicelli (Washington), Michael A. Osborn (Kalamazoo), Robert M. Miller (Pittsburgh), Rev. William M. Ogrodowski (Vice-Rector), Rev. Msgr. Edwin F. O'Brien (Rector), William P. Siple (Pittsburgh), Joseph G. Fonti (Brooklyn), Thomas P. Chester (Trenton)

Second Row: Liam Cary (Portland, OR), Phillip A. Altavilla (Scranton), William J. Waltersheid (Harrisburg), David Nott (Richmond), Mark K. Merkel (Omaha), Thomas J. Nelson (Washington), Joseph Pierce (Washington), Paul D. Etienne, II (Indianapolis), Joseph R. Chapel (Newark)

Third Row: James F. Checchio, III (Camden), Brian F. McGrath (Springfield), Thomas A. Milota (Joliet), Brian C. Hayes (San Diego), Christopher J. Kirwan (Boston), Michael F. Dogali (Bridgeport), Donald E. Henke (St. Louis), Edward K. Fisher (Memphis), Patrick J. Tomko (Chicago), Brian D. Hipp (Dodge City)

◀ CLASS OF 1993

Front Row: Allen Sanchez (Santa Fe), Vince Rogers (Kansas City-St. Joseph), Paul Zoghby (Mobile), Thomas Pomeroy (Green Bay), Rev. Msgr. Bernard E. Yarrish (Vice Rector for Administration), Rev. Msgr. Edwin O'Brien (Rector), Rev. Msgr. William Ogrodowski (Vice Rector for Student Life), Kent Kaufman (Toledo), Patrick Schumacher (Bismarck), Joseph Mulroney (Raleigh), Austin Vetter (Bismarck)

Second Row: John Byrnes (Altoona-Johnstown), Mark Thomas (Pittsburgh), Edward Byerley (Camden), Chester Murtha (Sioux Falls), Jaime Escobedo (San Diego), Steven Biegler (Rapid City), Rory Pitstick (Spokane), Enrique Lopez (Las Cruces), John McHugh (La Crosse), John O'Connor (Brooklyn), Daniel Vallecorsa (Pittsburgh), Thomas Haberkern (St. Louis), Scott Patt (Scranton), William Byrne (Washington), Edward McNulty (San Diego), Jay Scott Newman (Charleston), James Steffes (Winona), Brian Shimon (Green Bay), Jeffrey Monforton (Detroit)

◀ CLASS OF 1994

Front Row: Gregory Salata (Memphis), Leo Walsh (Anchorage), Rev. Msgr. William Ogrodowski (Vice Rector for Student Life), Rev. Msgr. Edwin F. O'Brien (Rector), Rev. Msgr. Bernard E. Yarrish (Vice Rector for Administration), Richard Reidy (Worcester), Michael Caridi (Pittsburgh)

Second Row: James Curry (Chicago), Mark Chimiak (Washington), Michael Champagne (Lafayette), Albert Kenney (Providence), Robert Gruss (Davenport), Marcel Taillon (Providence)

Third Row: Gary Studniewski (Washington), Todd Lajiness (Detroit), John Lendvai (Pittsburgh), Mark Hamilton (Louisville), George Stewart (New York), James Rafferty (Scranton), Christopher Hartshorn (Des Moines), Paul Murphy (Bridgeport)

◀ CLASS OF 1995

Front Row: James Wehner (Pittsburgh), Michael Farmer (Mobile), Rev. Msgr. William Ogrodowski (Vice Rector for Student Life), Rev. Msgr. Timothy M. Dolan (Rector), Rev. Msgr. Bernard E. Yarrish (Vice Rector for Administration), Joseph Dorner (Green Bay), Barry Hudock (Erie), Gregory Rothfuchs (Joliet)

Second Row: Gregory Benassu (Atlanta), Mark Lacey (Atlanta), Nicholas Cirillo (Bridgeport), Paul Eversole (Arlington), Mark DiFabio (Springfield), Todd Molinari (Portland, OR), Gary Linsky (Charleston), Michael Baumgardner (San Diego), Matthew Hoover (Columbus)

Third Row: Patrick Dolan (Denver), Paul McDuffie (Charleston), Paul Griffin (Bridgeport), Jack Gleason (Tulsa), Robert Panke (Washington), Edward Fitzgerald (Charleston), James Kee (Mobile), John Chadwick (Newark)

CLASS OF 1996 ▶

FRONT ROW: Gregory Beaumont (Fresno), John Anderson (Atlanta), Rev. Msgr. William Ogrodowski (Vice Rector for Student Life), Rev. Msgr. Timothy M. Dolan (Rector), Rev. Msgr. Bernard E. Yarrish (Vice Rector for Administration), Earl Eggleston (San Diego), Marc Swartvagher (Brooklyn), Andrew Kilpatrick (Scranton)

SECOND ROW: Michael Johnston (Portland, OR), John Andrews (Omaha), Christopher Ciccarino (Newark), Andrew Beerman (Winona), Anthony Wolf (La Crosse), Robert Spezia (Detroit), Andrew King (New York), Brian Gannon (Bridgeport), Eric Berns (La Crosse), Stephen Nash (Washington)

THIRD ROW: David Sizemore (Columbus), Michael Robinson (San Diego), Bernard Shlesinger, III (Raleigh), Christopher Murphy (Arlington), Michael Rodriguez (El Paso), John Riccardo (Detroit), Timothy Keeney (Richmond), Thomas Richter (Bismarck), Paul Scalia (Arlington)

CLASS OF 1997 ▶

FRONT ROW: Kenneth J. Malley (St. Petersburg), Dougald J. McCallum (Helena), Rev. Msgr. William Ogrodowski (Vice Rector for Student Life), Rev. Msgr. Timothy M. Dolan (Rector), Br. Randal Riede, C.F.X. (Librarian), Rev. Msgr. Bernard E. Yarrish (Vice Rector for Administration), Thomas E. Cook (Winona), Walter Ray Williams (Charlotte)

SECOND ROW: Robert W. Dillon (New York), Jason A. Gray (Peoria), James A. Teti (Newwark), David T. Toups (St. Petersburg), James M. Williams (Colorado Springs), Timothy P. McKeown (Savannah), Thomas W. Powers, Jr. (Bridgeport), Scott J. A. Buchanan (Charleston), Joseph L. Villa (Indianapolis), Richard D. Wilson (Fall River), Patrick E. Dempsey (Washington), Mark D. Knestout (Washington)

THIRD ROW: Rodolfo G. Garcia (Dallas), Daniel J. Maurer (Pittsburgh), Peter M. Idler (Camden), Stephen M. Cook (Kansas City-St. Joseph), Antonio G. Dittmer (Peoria), Wayne V. Sattler (Bismarck), Daniel J. Jones (Detroit), K. Bartholomew Smith (Washington), James H. Hauver (Duluth), Richard Kien-Ming Au (Vancouver), Paul N. Check (Bridgeport)

CLASS OF 1998 ▶

FRONT ROW: Robert J. Jaskot (Baltimore), Stephen J. Schreiber (Erie), Rev. Msgr. William Ogrodowski (Vice Rector for Student Life), Rev. Msgr. Timothy M. Dolan (Rector), Rev. Msgr. Bernard E. Yarrish (Vice Rector for Administration), John P. Cush (Brooklyn), Eric C. Phillips (Rochester), Christopher J. Pollard (Arlington)

SECOND ROW: Hòa Trung Trân (Atlanta), Bryan L. Hersey (Seattle), Bryan D. Patterson (Brooklyn), Kent F. Drotar (Denver), Samsaim P. Bianchi (Bridgeport), Blaise R. Berg (Sacramento), Jeffrey D. Burrill (La Crosse), Joseph R. Johnson (St. Paul-Minneapolis)

THIRD ROW: John M. Torrez (Kansas City, KS), Daniel J. Merz (Jefferson City), Erik T. Pohlmeier (Little Rock), John R. Cihak (Portland, OR), David R. Lefort (Albany), David E. Stevens (Sioux Falls), Paul Broussard (Lafayette, LA), Stephen E. Martin (Mobile)

◀ CLASS OF 1999

FRONT ROW: Chistopher Nalty (New Orleans), Leo Patalinghug (Baltimore), Robert McClory (Detroit), Sam Martin (La Crosse), Rev. Msgr. William Ogrodowski (Vice Rector for Student Life), Rev. Msgr. Timothy M. Dolan (Rector), Rev. Msgr. Bernard E. Yarrish (Vice Rector for Administration), Matthew Furey (New York), Tam Xuan Tran (Washington), Mark Vander Steeg (Green Bay), Gregory Parkes (Orlando)

SECOND ROW: Daniel Gallagher (Gaylord), Paul Halladay (Mobile), Peter Harman (Springfield, IL), James Csaszar (Columbus), James Bahash (San Diego), Keith Streifel (Bismarck), Thaddeus McGuire (Phoenix), Brian Christensen (Rapid City), Roger Landry (Fall River), Erik Arnold (Baltimore), Robert Moses (Orlando), Stephen Hamilton (Oklahoma City)

THIRD ROW: Ryan Lewis (Omaha), Mickey McGrath (Rochester), Andrew Semler (Dallas), Gary Benz (Bismarck), Terrence Brennan (Santa Fe), Richard McDonald (Kansas City, KS), Anthony Generose (Scranton), Tadeusz Pacholczyk (Fall River), Matthew Carr (Arlington), Joel Hastings (Duluth), Joseph Betschart (Portland, OR), Peter Lynch (Bridgeport)

CLASS OF 2000

FRONT ROW: Alejandro E. Valladares (Mobile), Dennis Michael Garcia (Santa Fe), José Juan Serna (Stockton), Michael John Lynam (Pittsburgh), Rev. Msgr. Bernard E. Yarrish (Vice Rector for Administration), Rev. Msgr. Timothy M. Dolan (Rector), Rev. Edward Smith (Vice-Rector), Victor Michael Blazovich (Spokane), John Paul Kimes (Eparchy of Our Lady of Lebanon), Raymond Joseph LaVoie (Harrisburg), John Adam Sistare (Providence), David William Whalen (Pittsburgh), Stephen Andrew Hero (Edmonton), Kristian Caelum Teater (St. Louis)

SECOND ROW: Thomas George Lahood (Washington), Michael Allen Dodd (Tulsa), James Bernard John Farnan (Pittsburgh), Derek J. Lappe (Seattle), Daniel Joseph Barnett (Spokane), Jeffery Scott Loseke (Omaha), Gerard Peter O'Connor (Fall River), Luke Richard Ballman (Atlanta), Joel Edward Cycenas (St. Paul and Minneapolis), Joseph Wilfred Giroux. Jr. (Ogdensberg), Thomas King Connolly III (Spokane), Jason Carl Crossen (Davenport), Charles Arthur Byrd, Jr. (Atlanta), Todd Anthony Kreitinger (Mobile)

THIRD ROW: Paul C. Carman (Syracuse), Thomas George Sinnott (Scranton), Timothy Edward MacDonald (Lansing), Bryce A. Sibley (Lafayette), Scott S. Traymor (Sioux Falls), Ronald Thomas Kunkel (Chicago), Adam J. Parker (Baltimore), Jeffrey Walter Wilborn (Denver), William G. Rice (Erie), Francisco Q. Flores (Boise), Steven Warner Bird (Peoria), David M. Shoemaker (Mobile)

CLASS OF 2001 ▶

FRONT ROW: Rev. William J. Waltersheid (Vice Rector for Student Life), Scott F. Boone (Dubuque), Eric C. Weber (Lansing), Msgr. Timothy M. Dolan (Rector), Trevor K. Murry (Belleville), Michael D. Irwin (Mobile), Rev. Msgr. Kevin C. McCoy (Vice Rector for Administration)

SECOND ROW: J. Patrick Serna (Corpus Christi), Martin E. Flum (Washington), Christopher A. Layden (Peoria), Steven J. Lopes (San Francisco), Christopher S. Sahd (Scranton), Luke M. Sweeney (New York), James M. Poumade (Arlington), F. John Ringley (Bridgeport)

THIRD ROW: Kevin M. Bazzel (Birmingham), David A. Pignato (Fall River), Brian D. Chadwick (Gary), James A. Tucker (Arlington), Brian T. Waldbillig (La Crosse), Rodney E. Thibault (Fall River), Hongshik Don Bosco Park (Newark), James P. Morgan (Sioux Falls)

FOURTH ROW: Jason M. Labbé (Baton Rouge), Thomas N. Haber (Bridgeport), Richard J. Toohey (Erie), Frank D. Epperson (Santa Rosa), Michael A. Colello (Providence), John K. Mark (St. Thomas in the Virgin Islands), James R. Bartylla (Madison)

NOT PICTURED: James E. Mason (Sioux Falls)

Class of 2002 ▶

Front Row: David Desmond (Sioux Falls), Joseph Lopez (Corpus Christi), Felipe Pulido (Yakima), Tait Schroeder (Madison), Justin Martin (Indianapolis), Rev. William Waltersheid (Vice Rector), Msgr. Kevin C. McCroy (Rector), Santiago Raudes Noguera (Sacramento), David Espinal (Brooklyn), Bradley Pelzel (Sioux City), Raymond de Souza (Kingston), Joshua Rodrigue (Nouma-Thibodaux)

Second Row: Dũng Nguyên (Atlanta), Dean Perri (Providence), Mark Reeves (Miami), Paul Rutten (Sioux Falls), Benjamin Dallas (Savannah), Timothy McMorland (Washington), John Gizler (Pittsburgh), George Healy (Miami), Edward Yew (Tulsa), Abel Mena-Lopez (Santa Rosa), Henry Huber (Dubuque), Paul Hoesing (Omaha), Michael Keating (St. Paul-Minneapolis), Brian Clarke (Scranton)

Third Row: Adam Hertzfeld (Toledo), John Fleckenstein (Kalamazoo), Dennis Yurochko (Pittsburgh), Paul Fontanella (Scranton), Jason Rocks (Camden), Robert Horihan (Winona), Theodore Book (Atlanta), Roberto Cortes-Campos (Washington), James Shea (Bismark), Brian Klingele (Kansas City, KS), Corey Belden (St. Paul-Minneapolis), Erik Walters (Mobile), Joseph Fowler (Pensacola-Tallahassee)

Not Pictured: Michael Patullo (Duluth), Msgr. Mark Svarczkopf (Vice Rector), Christiaan Kappes (Indianapolis), Scott Sunnenberg (Springfield-Cape Girardeau)

Class of 2003 ▶

Front Row: Evelio Manjivar-Ayala (Washington), Jeffrey Molnar (Pittsburgh), Rev. William Waltersheid (Vice Rector for Student Life), Rev. Msgr. Kevin C. McCoy (Rector), Rev. Msgr. Mark Svarczkopf (Vice Rector for Administration), Daniel Walz (St. Cloud), T. Austin Murphy (Baltimore)

Second Row: Shane Baxter (Beaumont), Miguel De Angel-Ramirez (Caguas), Gregory Coan (Washington), Michael Nguyen (Orange, CA), Trần Thanh Tùng (Corpus Christi), Edward Horkan (Arlington), Kenneth Wasilewski (Rockford), Matthew La Chance (Tulsa), Jacobo Muñoz (Rapid City)

Third Row: Paul Czerwonka (La Crosse), Patrick Moses (Orange, CA), Thomas Szydlik (Peoria), Christopher Singer (Erie), Martin De Mayo (Bridgeport), Walter Tad Oxley (Toledo), Robert Golas (Washington), Matthew Buening (Baltimore), Bryann Stitt (Ogdensburg), Timothy Riley (Providence)

Fourth Row: Todd Reitmeyer (Sioux Falls), John Reiley (Kansas City, KS), Kevin Magner (St. Paul-Minneapolis), Kevin Martin (Portland, ME), Jonathan Meyer (Indianapolis), Robert Forcier (Providence), J. D. Jaffe (Arlington), Kevin Achbach (Rapid City)

◄ CLASS OF 2004

FRONT ROW: Michael DeAscanis (Baltimore), Matthew Glover (Providence), John Rozembajgier (Metuchen), Rev. Peter McGuine (Vice Rector for Student Life), Rev. Msgr. Kevin C. McCoy (Rector), Rev. Msgr. James F. Checchio (Vice Rector for Administration), Terrence Walsh (Bridgeport), Carter Griffin (Washington), Daniel Straughn (Pittsburgh)

SECOND ROW: Thomas Fitzpatrick (Sioux Falls), Brian Sanderfoot (Washington), Peter Cipriani (Bridgeport), Joseph Craddock (Providence), Joshua Wagner (Columbus), Jeffrey Lorig (Omaha), Christopher Mahar (Providence), Jeremy Secrist (Jefferson City), Nicholas March (Dubuque)

THIRD ROW: Shane Kirby (Scranton), Daniel Firmin (Savannah), Thomas Kunz (Pittsburgh), Christopher Floss (Joliet), Lam Le (Grand Rapids), Thomas Henner (Davenport), Justin Wachs (Sioux Falls), Matthew Hewitt (Sioux City), Qui-Thac Nguyen (Seattle), Ronald Richards (Detroit)

NOT PICTURED: Nate Sokol (Lansing)

◄ CLASS OF 2005

FRONT ROW: Michael Vuky (Portland, OR), Rev. Peter McGuine (Vice Rector for Student Life), Rev. Msgr. Kevin C. McCoy (Rector), Rev. Msgr. James F. Checchio (Vice Rector for Administration), Mark Steffl (New Ulm), William Vit (Sioux City), Mark Reburiano (San Francisco)

SECOND ROW: James David Carter (Knoxville), Craig Timmerman (New Ulm), John Gallas (St. Paul-Minneapolis), Adam Park (Washington), Donald Libby (Gaylord), Jason Makos (Boston), Brian Dellaert (Dubuque), Bob Poitras (Boston), Joseph Freeman (San Diego), Anthony Lonzo (Columbus), Stephen Doktorczyk (Orange, CA), Karl C. Bissinger (Fall River), Randy Fronek (Rockford), Jason Tyler (Little Rock), Justin Fish (Duluth), Gerald Goodrum (Galveston-Houston), Daniel Hanley (Arlington), Eric F. Hastings (Duluth)

FRONT ROW: Justin Ferguson (Savannah), Craig Haider (San Diego), Avelino Gonzalez (Washington), Rev. Peter McGuine (Vice Rector for Student Life), Rev. Msgr. James F. Checchio (Rector), Mark Lenneman (Helena), James Lease (Harrisburg), Anthony Ouellette (Kansas City, KS), Joseph Redfern (La Crosse)

SECOND ROW: Patrick Peach (Baltimore), Christopher Washington (Scranton), Jeremy Letherby (Sacramento), John Barno (Newark), Raymond Enzweiler (Covington), Shawn Conoboy (Youngstown), James Richardson (St. Philip Neri House, Kalamazoo), Daniel Wathen (Great Falls-Billings), Robert Keighron (Brooklyn), Joseph Campbell (Erie), John Delaney (Camden)

THIRD ROW: Timothy Hall (Winona), Harold Reeves (Washington), Joel Sember (Green Bay), Jason Vidrine (Lafayette), Brian Needles (Newark), Michael McLane (Trenton), Joseph Shetler (Jefferson City), Phillip Cozzi (Arlington), Benjamin Sember (Green Bay), Tyler Miller (Springfield, IL), Joshua Brommer (Harrisburgh), David Grondz (St. Philip Neri House, Kalamazoo)

CLASS OF 2007 ▶

FRONT ROW: Aaron J. Kuhn (St. Cloud), Michael R. Ruffalo (Pittsburgh), Christopher R. Frazer (Sacramento), Jay Mello (Fall River), Rev. Peter McGuine (Vice Rector for Student Life), Rev. Msgr. James F. Checchio (Rector), Rev. Msgr. Daniel H. Mueggenborg (Vice Rector for Administration), Aaron D. Killips (Savannah), John G. McDonald (Birmingham), Richard J. Schamber (Pensacola-Tallahasse), Seamus P. Griesbach (Portland, OR)

SECOND ROW: Joseph J. Shimek (Milwaukee), Isaac Orozco (Fort Worth), Michael P. Cassaban (Charleston), Joshua P. Guillory (Lafayette), Lucas E. Tomson (Spokane), Bryan P. Babick (Charleston), Michael M. Romano (Camden), Ronald R. Nelson, Jr. (Portland, OR), Alejandro Del Toro (Rockford), Jaime D. Rivera-Cortijo (Atlanta), Kim J. Schreck (Pittsburgh), Joshua K. Waltz (Bismarck)

THIRD ROW: Kenneth T. St. Hilaire (Spokane), David J. Ruchinski (St. Augustine), John J. O'Brien (St. Louis), Jason B. Cargo (Dallas), Michael S. Triplett (Baltimore), James J. Peak (Spokane), Ryan M. Bredemeyer (Peoria), Jeffrey F. Kirby (Charleston), Michael A. Carlson (Hartford), Andrew J. Keswick (Melbourne), Andrew J. Roza (Omaha)

FOURTH ROW: Joseph E. Rogers (Washington), Peter J. Pupura (Brooklyn), Zachary J. Weber (Cincinnati), Christopher G. Roberts (Lafayette, IN)

CLASS OF 2008 ▶

Front Row: Samuel S. Kachuba (Bridgeport), Vincent J. DeRosa (Washington), Jeremy J. Rodrigues (Providence), Rev. Msgr. Daniel H. Mueggenborg (Vice Rector for Administration), Rev. Msgr. James F. Checchio (Rector), Rev. Msgr. Robert D. Gruss (Vice Rector for Seminary Life), Nicholas Dudo (Camden), Mark D. Glover (Springfield, MA), Kevin J. Regan (Washington)

Second Row: Edison M. Tayag (Rochester), Thomas M. Neuhaus (Winona), Nicholas J. Argentieri (Pittsburgh), Julio A. Vincent Orellana (Boise), Paul J. Fasano (Rockford), Jonathon L. Reardon (Springfield, MA), Ryan J. Moravitz (Duluth), Justin J. Kizewski (La Crosse), David G. Thurber (Providence)

Third Row: Nicolas Maurice (Lismore), Shane A. Deman (Sioux City), Gregory F. Loughney (Scranton), Robert D. Lampitt (Peoria), Joseph M. Freedy (Pittsburgh), Matthew J. Nicks (Spokane), Patrick J. Riffle, Jr. (Washington), Steven M. Titus (Cheyenne), Ronald P. Floyd (Fall River)

◀ CLASS OF 2009

Front Row: Jesse Burish (La Crosse), Adam Rust (Memphis), Joshua Ehli (Bismarck), Rev. Msgr. Daniel H. Mueggenborg (Vice-Rector for Administration), Rev. Msgr. James F. Checchio (Rector), Rev. Msgr. Robert D. Gruss (Vice-Rector for Seminary Life), Gregory Rannazzisi (Rockville Centre), David Kuttner (Spokane), Albert Marcello III (Providence)

Second Row: Pablo Migone (Savannah), Jeffrey Droessler (Orange), Roberto Ortiz (Newark), Sean Danda (Indianapolis), Edward D'Almeida (Little Rock), Dishan Candappa (Melbourne), Daniel Champoli (Brooklyn), Justin Bianchi (Venice), Charles Cortinovis (Washington), Ernest Cibelli (Baltimore)

Third Row: Aaron Esch (Milwaukee), Robert Mucci (Brooklyn), Joshua Stevens (Wheeling-Charleston), Nicholas Azar II (Atlanta), Thomas Kelly (Venice), Ryan Erlenbush (Great Falls-Billings), James Melnick (Little Rock), Theodore Lange (Portland, OR)

Fourth Row: James Adams (Kalamazoo), Nick Schneider (Bismarck), James McCarthy (Sydney), Nicholas Vaskov (Pittsburgh), Joseph Previtali (San Francisco), Gerald Shantillo (Scranton), Robert Wagner (Arlington), James DeViese (Wheeling-Charleston)

◀ CLASS OF 2010

FRONT ROW: Llane Briese (Atlanta), Charles Gallagher (Washington, D.C.), Adam Young (Providence), Jason Schumer (St. Louis), Rev. Msgr. Daniel Mueggenborg, Rev. Msgr. James Checchio, Rev. Msgr. Robert Gruss, Efrain Bautista (San Diego), Nolan Lowry (Tyler), Daniel O'Mullane (Patterson), Paul Carlson (Peoria)

SECOND ROW: Michael Novajosky (Bridgeport), Scott Pogatchnik (St. Cloud), Christopher Cicero (Youngstown), Nicholas Bellotti (Newark), Andrew James (Sydney), Nicholas Desimone (Worcester), Justin Huber (Washington, D.C.), David Rivera (Camden), Jacob Bertrand (San Diego), Gregory Ihm (Madison), Luke Austin (Burlington), Vincent Arong (Galveston-Houston), John Burns (Milwaukee), James Morrison (Mobile), John Sheridan (Youngstown), Jeremy Trowbridge (Rockford)

THIRD ROW: Joshua Stengel (Little Rock), David Schunk (San Francisco), Michael Bruno (Brooklyn), Peter Finney III (New Orleans), Brian Noel (Pittsburgh), Fernando Sáenz (Santa Fe), Ian McDole (Covington), Chase Hasenoehrl (Boise), Matthew Kuhn (St. Cloud), Michael Silloway (Atlanta), Dwight Schlaline (Harrisburg), Anthony Lickteig (Washington, D.C.), Matthew Bartulica (Kansas City-St. Joseph), Matthew Wiering (New Ulm), David Carrano (Madison), Craig Vasek (Crookston), Frederick Boni (Mobile)

◀ PRESENT THIRD THEOLOGY CLASS

FRONT ROW: Cory Stanley (Oklahoma City), Ryan Creamer (Rockville Centre), Brandon Bernhard (Tyler), Paul Vu (Orange, CA), Rheo Ofalsa (Omaha), Jeffrey Eirvin (Portland, OR), Jeffrey Starkovich (Lake Charles), Mark Payton (Perth)

SECOND ROW: Christopher Markman (Fargo), Aaron Johanneck (New Ulm), William Brunner (Green Bay), Adam Verona (Pittsburgh), Riley Williams (Fall River), James Yamauchi (Dallas), Neal Hock (Grand Island), Anthony Craig (Duluth)

THIRD ROW: Peter Zwaans (Adelaide), Nathan Sparks (Rapid City), Richard Mastrogiacomo (Rockville Centre), Jorge Cespedes (Memphis), Aaron Rose (Sacramento), Quan Tran (Orange, CA), James Baron (Colorado Springs), Joseph McQuaide IV (Wilmington)

FOURTH ROW: Christopher Donley (Pittsburgh), Michael Pratt (Tulsa), James Dodson (Burlington), H. Ray Cho (Newark), George Nixon (Providence), David Nerbun (Charleston)

FIFTH ROW: Stephen Vrazel (Mobile), Anthony Kruse (Dubuque), E. Theodore Martin (Kalamazoo), William Ruelle (Bismarck), Keith Romke (Rockford), Travis Burnett (Mobile)

SIXTH ROW: Matthew Libra (Portland, OR), John Solomon (Wilmington), Philip Zubrod (Fargo)

NOT PICTURED: Jonathan P. Bakkelund (Rockford), Sean Donovan (Tulsa), Philip A. Smith (Toledo), Brian J. Soliven (Sacramento)

PRESENT SECOND THEOLOGY CLASS ▶

FRONT ROW: Alex Roche (Scranton), Stephen Giulietti (Brooklyn), Andrew Hart (Little Rock), Jay Bananal (San Diego), Lam Hoang (Galveston-Houston), Patrick Arensburg (Mobile)

SECOND ROW: James Wallace (Chicago), Thomas Gallagher (Wheeling-Charleston), Andrew Henrick (Santa Fe), Francis Marotti (Kalamazoo), Luke Millette (Galveston-Houston), Mario Majano (Washington, D.C.), David Martinez (Venice), Nicholas Rynne (Sydney), Brian Frice (San Diego), Donald Anstoetter (St. Louis), Corey Close (Davenport), Alan Dietzenbach (Dubuque), Giancarlo Pattugalan (Brooklyn), Adam Haake (Kansas City-St. Joseph)

THIRD ROW: Samuel Spiering (Great Falls-Billings), Joseph Zwosta (Brooklyn), Andrew Young (Sioux Falls), Matthew Grady (Venice), Carmelo Morales (Amarillo), Michael Sedar (Pittsburgh)

FOURTH ROW: David Tedesche (Rochester), Frederick Gruber (Pittsburgh), Eric Bennett (Boston), Jadyn Nelson (Bismarck)

FIFTH ROW: Philip Halladay (Mobile), Patrick Lewis (Washington, D.C.), Adam Johnson (Kansas City-St. Joseph), Jason Adams (Savannah), Michael Gallacher (Melbourne), Joseph Bergida (Arlington), Colin Wen (Sacramento), Mark Miller (Madison)

SIXTH ROW: Victor Ingalls (Mobile), Benjamin Danielson (Rockford), Benjamin Jones (Alexandria), Robert Shea (Bismarck), Jeffery Walker (Toledo), Ryan Connors (Providence), Jacob Strand (Milwaukee)

SEVENTH ROW: Anthony Dill (Harrisburg), Jeremy Vidmar (Duluth), Daniel Weiske (Duluth), Benjamin Ross (Gary), Derrick Oliveria (Oakland), Matthew Kraemer (Fargo), David Santos (Newark), James Mangan (Lansing), Michael Isenburg (Arlington), Daniel Kirk (Trenton), Brian Romportl (Green Bay)

PRESENT FIRST THEOLOGY CLASS ▶

FRONT ROW: Michael Casey (Hartford), Christopher Seiler (St. Louis), David Esquiliano-Diaz (Sioux City), Thomas McNally (Kalamazoo), Nicholas Barnes (Arlington)

SECOND ROW: Justin Raines (Nashville), Simon Carian (Santa Fe), Francisco Aguirre (Washington, D.C.), Michael Garry (Duluth), Charles Samson (St. Louis), Brian Buettner (Oklahoma City)

THIRD ROW: Daniel Ulishney (Greensburg), Michael Cornell (Perth), Preston Huck (Pittsburgh), John Lovitsch (Joliet), Douglas Marcotte (Indianapolis), Jun Hee Lee (Brooklyn), Matthew Morelli (Greensburg)

FOURTH ROW: Elias Gieske (Duluth), Martin Rodriguez (Indianapolis), Brian Baker (Atlanta), Brandon Macadaeg (Oakland), Nicholas Nelson (Duluth), Joseph Langan (Baltimore), Thomas Macdonald (Boston)

FIFTH ROW: Timothy Daniel (Washington, D.C.), John Norman (Omaha), Alan Guanella (Lacrosse), Peter Van Lieshout (Rochester), Spencer Howe (Minneapolis-St. Paul), John Connaughton (Bridgeport)

SIXTH ROW: Kinneth Easter (Nashville), Jason Christian (Charlotte), Christopher Little (Baltimore), Brendan Bartlett (Arlington), Ryan Browning (Rockford), Joseph Laracy (Newark), Scott Jablonsky (Madison)

SEVENTH ROW: James Platania (Paterson), Matthew Stehling (Tyler), Brennan Sia (Perth), Michael Pawlowicz (Joliet), Daniel McCaughan (Sydney), Daniel Gallagher (Pittsburgh), Christopher Gray (Salt Lake City)

EIGHTH ROW: Jason Doke (Jefferson City), Damian Jellett (Wagga Wagga), Krzystof Kuczynski (Bridgeport), Michael Pierz (Springfield, MA), Peter Heasley (New York), Eric Scanlan (Venice), Christopher Heanue (Brooklyn), John Gibson (Milwaukee)

Rectors of the North American College

Through the leadership, influence and legacy of its Rectors, the North American College has continued its mission to provide for the Church in North America happy, healthy and holy priests with a love and appreciation for the Successor of St. Peter and broad understanding of the issues the world faces in following Christ.

"THIS EXPERIENCE IN ROME REVEALS THE BROADER EXPERIENCE OF THE CATHOLIC CHURCH AS A UNIVERSAL EXPRESSION OF OUR FAITH IN JESUS CHRIST."

-- MSGR. KEVIN MCCOY, '81, C'86, RECTOR 2001-2005

"FOR SEVEN YEARS, I HAD TO PINCH MYSELF DAILY, WONDERING IF SERVING AS RECTOR OF THE COLLEGE THAT HAD ENCHANTED ME AS A SEMINARIAN WAS JUST A DREAM. THOSE YEARS WERE SO FORMATIVE, AND MY OWN PRIESTHOOD WAS INSPIRED BY HUNDREDS OF YOUNG MEN WHO WERE PREPARED AS PRIESTS AT THE COLLEGE, BY PRIESTS WHO CAME AS GRADUATE STUDENTS OR ON SABBATICAL, BY DEVOTED FACULTY, AND BY THE TOWERING PRESENCE OF JOHN PAUL II. AND NOW, ON MADISON AVENUE, WHEN I DREAM . . . I DREAM OF HER, THE COLLEGE I LOVE."

-- ARCHBISHOP TIMOTHY DOLAN, '76, RECTOR 1994-2001

"AN AMERICAN STUDYING ABROAD TAKES ON A WHOLE NEW PERSPECTIVE, HIS MIND IS OPENED ALL THE MORE. THERE IS ONE CATHOLIC FAITH, BUT WE ARE ABLE TO UNDERSTAND WHAT THAT ONE FAITH MEANS IN A VARIETY OF HUMAN EXPERIENCES. THAT'S THE BLESSING OF AN AMERICAN SEMINARIAN PREPARING FOR THE PRIESTHOOD AT THE NORTH AMERICAN COLLEGE."

-- MSGR. LAWRENCE PURCELL, '66, C'74, RECTOR 1984-1990

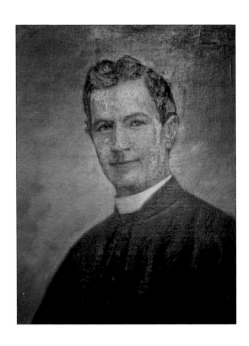

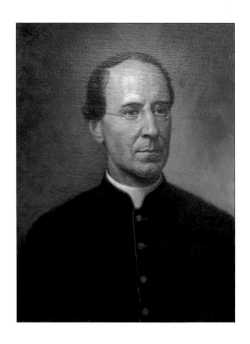

Bernard Smith O.S.B.
1859-1860

William G. McCloskey
1860-1868

Silas M. Chatard
1868-1878

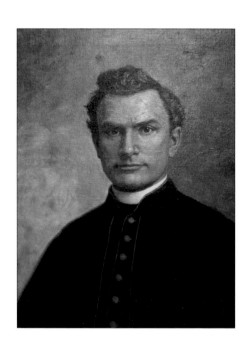

Louis E. Hostlot
1878-1884

Augustin J. Schulte
1884-1885

Denis J. O'Connell
1885-1895

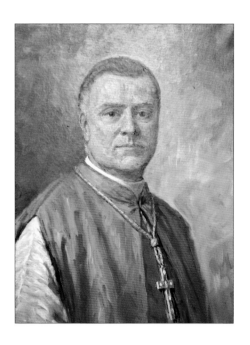

William H. O'Connell
1895-1901

Thomas F. Kennedy
1901-1917

Charles A. O'Hern
1917-1925

Eugene S. Burke
1925-1935

Ralph L. Hayes
1935-1944

J. Gerald Kealy
1945-1946

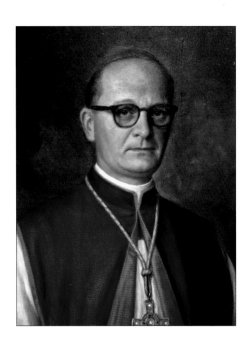

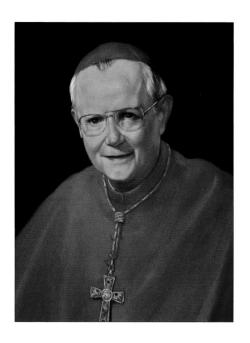

Martin J. O'Connor
1946-1964

Francis F. Reh
1964-1968

James A. Hickey
1969-1974

"IT'S REMARKABLE AND VERY GRATIFYING
TO SEE THE ROLE THAT OUR FORMER
STUDENTS HAVE IN THE CHURCH TODAY.
AN EXTRAORDINARY NUMBER HAVE TAKEN
ON RESPONSIBILITIES IN THE FORMATION
OF OTHER PRIESTS, WHICH SPEAKS TO THE
FORMATION THAT TAKES PLACE HERE, THE
PRIESTLY IDENTITY THAT IS GAINED AND OUR
VISION AND ZEAL FOR THE PRIESTHOOD."

-- ARCHBISHOP EDWIN O'BRIEN,
C'76, RECTOR 1990-1994

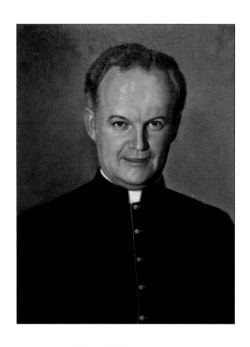

Harold P. Darcy
1974-1979

Charles M. Murphy
1979-1984

Lawrence M. Purcell
1984-1990

Edwin F. O'Brien
1990-1994

Timothy M. Dolan
1994-2001

Kevin C. McCoy
2001-2005

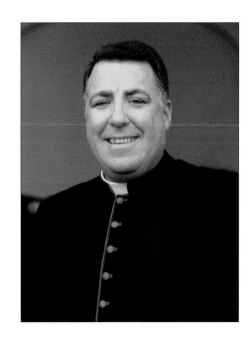

James F. Checchio
2005-Present

"Our seminarians and priests witness the importance of being a man in close conversation with the Lord through the example of our Holy Father. They hear first-hand the clarity with which he enunciates the teachings of Christ and His Church which is in part based on that solid relationship the Holy Father has with the Lord Himself."

-- Msgr. James Checchio,
'92, C'97, Rector since 2005

A Visit to the Alma Mater

The year-long celebration of the Sesquicentennial Anniversary culminated in a private audience with His Holiness, Pope Benedict XVI.

On January 9, 2010, the students, priests, faculty, staff and alumni of the North American College gathered in the Hall of Benedictions to participate in the momentous event. The Holy Father personally greeted all present and delivered an address to commemorate the historic milestone. His address included special remarks to the hundreds of alumni who had returned to Rome for a reunion hosted by the College, calling on them to remember with gratitude the time of their studies and renew their love for their Alma Mater.

"Your Holiness, the seminarians, student priests, alumni, and faculty of the College recall with gratitude your pastoral visit to the United States and continue to take to heart and prayer the many inspiring homilies and challenging messages you offered our brothers and sisters in the Lord who gathered to welcome you from across our great nation. We were particularly motivated by your encouraging words to the priests and seminarians in New York: "Strive for a pattern of life truly marked by charity, chastity and humility, in imitation of Christ, the Eternal High Priest, of whom you are to become living icons.""

-- Msgr. James Checchio, Rector, in his address presenting Pope Benedict XVI to the College community

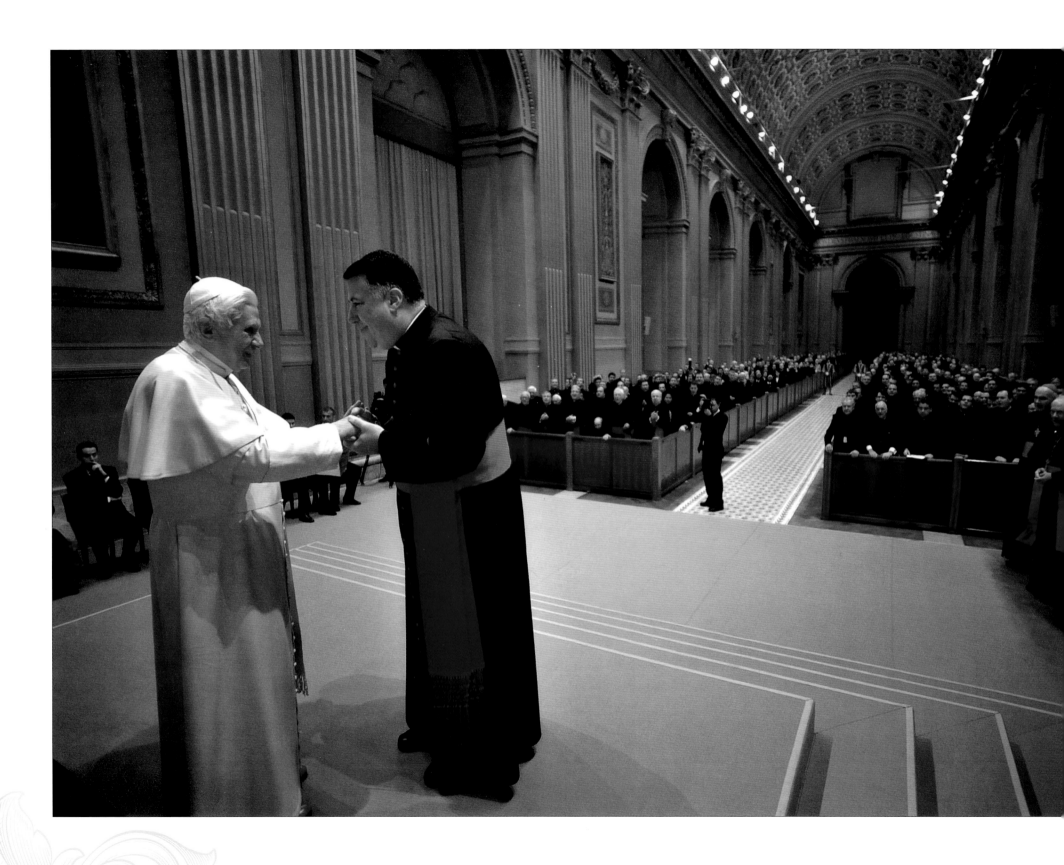

Address from His Holiness, Pope Benedict XVI

The Holy Father offered the following words during a private audience with the College community on January 9, 2010, concluding its 150th anniversary celebrations.

Your Eminences,

Dear Brother Bishops and Priests,

I am pleased to welcome the alumni of the Pontifical North American College, together with the Rector, faculty and students of the seminary on the Janiculum hill, and the student priests of the Casa Santa Maria dell' Umiltà. Our meeting comes at the conclusion of the celebrations marking the one hundred and fiftieth anniversary of the College's establishment by my predecessor, Blessed Pius IX. On this happy occasion I willingly join you in thanking the Lord for the many ways in which the College has remained faithful to its founding vision by training generations of worthy preachers of the Gospel and ministers of the sacraments, devoted to the Successor of Peter and committed to the building up of the Church in the United States of America.

It is appropriate, in this Year for Priests, that you have returned to the College and this Eternal City in order to give thanks for the academic and spiritual formation which has nourished your priestly ministry over the years. The present Reunion is an opportunity not only to remember with gratitude the time of your studies, but also to reaffirm your filial affection for the Church of Rome, to recall the apostolic labors of the countless alumni who have gone before you, and to recommit yourselves to the high ideals of holiness, fidelity and pastoral zeal which you embraced on the day of your ordination. It is likewise an occasion to renew your love for the College and your appreciation of its distinctive mission to the Church in your country.

During my Pastoral Visit to the United States, I expressed my conviction that the Church in America is called to cultivate "an intellectual 'culture' which is genuinely Catholic, confident in the profound harmony of faith and reason, and prepared to bring the richness of faith's vision to bear on the pressing issues which affect the future of American society" (Homily at Nationals Stadium, Washington, 17 April 2008). As Blessed Pius IX rightly foresaw, the Pontifical North American College in Rome is uniquely prepared to help meet this perennial challenge. In the century and a half since its foundation, the College has offered its students an exceptional experience of the universality of the Church, the breadth of her intellectual and spiritual tradition, and the urgency of her mandate to bring Christ's saving truth to the men and women of every time and place. I am confident that, by emphasizing these hallmarks of a Roman education in every aspect of its program of formation, the College will continue to produce wise and generous pastors capable of transmitting the Catholic faith in its integrity, bringing Christ's infinite mercy to the weak and the lost, and enabling America's Catholics to be a leaven of the Gospel in the social, political and cultural life of their nation.

Dear brothers, I pray that in these days you will be renewed in the gift of the Holy Spirit which you received on the day of your ordination. In the College chapel, dedicated to the Blessed Virgin Mary under the title of the Immaculate Conception, Our Lady is portrayed in the company of four outstanding models and patrons of priestly life and ministry: Saint Gregory the Great, Saint Pius X, Saint John Mary Vianney and Saint Vincent de Paul. During this Year for Priests, may these great saints continue to watch over the students who daily pray in their midst; may they guide and sustain your own ministry, and intercede for the priests of the United States. With cordial good wishes for the spiritual fruitfulness of the coming days, and with great affection in the Lord, I impart to you my Apostolic Blessing, which I willingly extend to all the alumni and friends of the Pontifical North American College.

Anniversary Year Events

The Pontifical North American College celebrated its Sesquicentennial Anniversary through a series of events. Each of these efforts expressed the life and ministry of priestly formation as it is currently experienced. These events included the following:

Sesquicentennial Anniversary Bell for the Casa Santa Maria

Since the College first opened its doors in 1859, the bell tower of the Humility Street campus has been missing one of its three bells. As part of the Sesquicentennial Anniversary and through the generous donation of an alumnus' home parish, the College was able to commission and install a finely-crafted bronze bell celebrating the anniversary year. The bell bears the coats of arms of the Holy Father, Pope Benedict XVI and the College. It also bears the anniversary years 1859-2009.

The bell was blessed in anticipation of the anniversary year by the Archbishop Edwin F. O'Brien, then-Chairman of the Board of Governors, at a Mass celebrated by Francis Cardinal George, President of the United States Conference of Catholic Bishops, with Monsignor James F. Checchio, Rector, and Monsignor Francis Kelly, Director of the Casa Santa Maria, as principal concelebrants.

Carl J. Peter Lecture by Archbishop Augustine DiNoia, OP

On December 7, 2008, the College formally initiated its anniversary celebration by welcoming Father J. Augustine DiNoia to address the community at the annual Carl J. Peter Lecture. His presentation focused on the dynamics of both the missionary and pastoral dimensions of evangelization as presented in the teachings of St. Paul. Such a topic was appropriate because the universal Church was celebrating the Pauline Year as well as the New Evangelization for which priests of the third millennium must be prepared. Archbishop DiNoia was subsequently ordained to the episcopacy on July 10, 2009. The College was honored to host the archbishop to celebrate a Mass of Thanksgiving on October 3, 2009, in the Chapel of the Immaculate Conception at the Janiculum campus.

Solemnity of the Immaculate Conception 2008

The first College liturgy celebrating the opening of the 150th anniversary year took place on December 8, 2008. His Eminence John Cardinal Foley, a long-time friend and alumnus, presided at the Mass and joined the community for the banquet afterwards. Cardinal Foley currently serves as the Grand Master of the Equestrian Order of the Holy Sepulchre of Jerusalem. In his homily, His Eminence reflected on the significant role the Blessed Virgin played in his own vocation and encouraged the community to consciously and prayerfully remain under the patronage of Our Lady.

Ad Multos Annos II DVD

With special gratitude for the generosity and professional expertise of Mr. Jack Ball, the College produced an informational DVD video celebrating its anniversary year and presenting its mission. This video is an important means of helping others understand the critical importance of priestly formation both before and after ordination in the Eternal City.

Regina Immaculata: Music in Honor of the Immaculate Conception Choir CD

In the spring of 2007, the College's choir recorded a CD of sacred music in honor of the Solemnity of the Immaculate Conception. The majority of the liturgical selections are from the Mass *Cum jubilo* by Maurice Duruflé, a late 19th century French composer. The CD showcases both the talent within the College community as well as the potential of the Mascioni pipe organ in the Chapel of the Immaculate Conception. It is the only professional recording of sacred music the College has ever undertaken. The CD was released at the beginning of the anniversary year in the winter of 2009.

The Institute for Priestly Formation Conference

The College hosted the eighth symposium on the Spirituality and Identity of the Diocesan Priest from February 22-25, 2009, at the Janiculum campus. The symposium's theme was "*Spiritual Fatherhood: Living Christ's Own Revelation of the Father*." The speakers were from the Institute of Priestly Formation at

Creighton University in Omaha, Nebraska, members of the College faculty, and Father Raniero Cantalamessa, O.F.M., Cap., Preacher of the Papal Household, who served as the keynote speaker.

Crucifix overlooking the Campo Sportivo

Through a generous gift of the Torolonia family and Massimiliano Mosca, the College recently received a beautiful outdoor crucifix which was originally crafted nearly 150 years ago and served as an outdoor devotional for a religious community living nearby on the Janiculum hill. This crucifix was restored and re-dedicated as part of the College campus during Lent 2009, thanks to the generosity of alumni from the Diocese of Providence, Rhode Island.

Pipe Organ for the Assumption Chapel

Through the generous support of alumni and friends, the College recently commissioned a new pipe organ for the Assumption Chapel which was installed in the spring of 2009. Designed and built by Mr. Robert Wech and his Munich-based company, the new organ will serve the liturgical music needs of the College for centuries to come. The organ was used for the first time during the Liturgy of the Lord's Passion on Palm Sunday, April 5, 2009.

Statue of Saint John Vianney, Patron of Priests

The Sesquicentennial Anniversary of the College partially coincides with the Year of the Priest proclaimed by Pope Benedict XVI. In honor of these events, a devotional statue of Saint John Vianney was commissioned by the College from the Ferdinand Stuflesser company in Ortisei and placed in the Chapel of the Immaculate Conception for veneration. Saint John Vianney had been previously established as the patron saint for parish priests; now, he is promoted as the patron of all priests. Through the establishment of this devotional statue, the College presents a visual reminder of the priestly example of the Curé of Ars for reflection and imitation in the lives of seminarians and priests.

Solemnity of the Immaculate Conception 2009

The College commemorated and celebrated the 150th anniversary of the actual first day of her existence. It was on December 7, 1859, that the first community of American seminarians processed from their residence at the Propagation of the Faith (*Piazza di Spagna*) to the front door of the house on Humility Street. The next day, December 8th, was the first full day of the College's life and ministry of priestly formation.

To assist us in celebrating this monumental day in our history, His Excellency, John J. Myers, Archbishop of Newark and Chairman of the Board of Governors, came to Rome to preside at the Anniversary Mass and joined the community at the banquet.

Alumni Reunion 2010

In January 2010, the College welcomed its alumni to a reunion hosted in Rome. More than 200 alumni were present for this reunion to mark the end of the Sesquicentennial Anniversary. One of the special events planned for the reunion was a return visit to the former Villa Santa Caterina near Castel Gandolfo – a place which is still remembered with affection by many alumni. During this reunion we were able to greet the Holy Father and thank him for the continuous support and encouragement of the Holy See for the College.

Pope Benedict XVI

The Latin inscription over the principal entrance of the College summarizes the filial respect and reverence for the Holy Father: *The young men who have come here from the distant shores of America, looking upon the Vatican Hill, strengthen their faith and their love for the Roman Pontiff.*

Since the College opened its doors 150 years ago, the various Popes have been particularly supportive and encouraging of its mission. Of particular note are the various visits and private audiences offered by Blessed Pius IX and the annual meetings of Pius X in which he addressed the seminarians saying, "*Without diminishing in the slightest my high regard for the many other national colleges in Rome, I have a special admiration for you, my dear young men, for you are truly my Benjamins, for whom I have the most tender affection.*" We also recall the encouragement of Pius XI to the American bishops inviting them to join with the Vatican in purchasing the Janiculum campus and the subsequent encouragement of Pius XII who asked the American bishops to re-open the College following World War II. With particular affection, esteem, and gratitude the College also recalls the personal visit of Pius XII who dedicated the new campus on October 14, 1953. Blessed John XXIII visited the College to commemorate the 100th anniversary of its founding in 1959 and Paul VI visited as well to commemorate the anniversary of the birth of George Washington. John Paul II visited the College twice during his papacy and frequently welcomed members of the college community in private audience.

The special unity between the Pontifical North American College and the Successor of Peter was demonstrated during a visit by John Paul II when he symbolically planted a California Redwood tree both at the Janiculum campus and in the Vatican Gardens.

His Holiness, Benedict XVI, is familiar with the North American College through his regular visits while serving as Cardinal Prefect of the Congregation for the Doctrine of the Faith. In 1999, he was the ordaining prelate for the College's diaconate ordination. Since his election, he frequently welcomes the New Men to Rome with his greetings at Castel Gandolfo as well as to the diaconandi and their families at St. Peter's. Recently, the Holy Father offered this encouragement, "I *welcome the new seminarians of the Pontifical North American College, and pray that their formative years in Rome will help them to grow in wisdom and pastoral charity.*"

The very portrait of the Holy Father which today is displayed in the refectory was personally blessed by His Holiness before being sent to the College. Each day, the community is blessed to gather with Pope Benedict XVI as our pastor and neighbor, father and friend.

Carl J. Peter Lecture by Archbishop Donald Wuerl

On January 10, 2010, the College hosted His Excellency, the Most Reverend Donald Wuerl, Archbishop of Washington, to offer the annual Carl J. Peter Lecture for the College community of alumni, current students, and guests.

Archbishop Wuerl is an accomplished theologian and distinguished leader of the Church in America as well as one of the College's most beloved and dedicated alumni. He recently served as a delegate for the Synod on the Word held in October 2008. His presentation focused on the work of that Synod and possible applications for the life of the Church. This event marked the conclusion of the sesquicentennial celebrations.

150th Anniversary Book

A 150th anniversary book documents both the College's history as well as its present life and ministry. This publication has been sent to every alumnus as well as the College's closest friends. The book is dedicated to His Holiness, Pope Benedict XVI, in appreciation for his personal friendship with the College.

PAGE 152: The 2010 Alumni Reunion brings together the six living Rectors of the College as well as Archbishop John J. Myers, Chairman of the Board of Governors, for the first time in the history of the institution.

PAGE 153: Signs of the demands of seminary life: a seminarian's work station in the Casa Santa Maria library.

PAGE 158: Surrounded by bishops and faculty, William Cardinal Levada, Prefect of the Congregation for the Doctrine of the Faith and graduate of the College, offers Mass in the Chapel of the Immaculate Conception for the College's 150th anniversary.

PAGE 159: A reminder of her past, the American flag is painted on the ceiling of the Villa Santa Caterina, the College's former summer residence.

PAGE 160: Msgr. Checchio greets Pope Benedict XVI on behalf of the College. The Rector offered the following words to the Holy Father: *"Holy Father, we pledge anew today our love and, above all, our prayers, for you. We again thank God for your leadership and priestly example, as well as for the special bond that we, as a Pontifical College, are privileged to share with you. As we pray that the Lord will continue to sustain you in your Petrine ministry, we hasten to ask as well for your apostolic blessing on those of us gathered here as well as on our families, benefactors and alumni whose pastoral responsibilities at home prevented them from joining us in Rome for this celebration. Holy Father, we love you; we pray for you; and we wish you ad multos annos!"*

LEFT: Archbishop Timothy Dolan, former Rector, preaches the opening Mass at the Church of the Twelve Apostles.

ABOVE: Faculty, student priests and alumni offer Mass in the Chapel of the Immaculate Conception with seminarians and friends of the College.

PAGE 166: A traditional *pranzone* was held in the refectory after the Anniversary Mass. Three traditional toasts were given, honoring the Holy Father, the United States and the College.

ABOVE LEFT: One of the longest serving members of the American Hierarchy, William Cardinal Baum was honored with the College's Founder's Award. Cardinal Baum, former Archbishop of Washington, D.C., has also served the Universal Church as Prefect of the Congregation for Catholic Education and Major Penitentiary of the Apostolic Penitentiary.

ABOVE RIGHT: Archbishop Donald Wuerl delivered the annual Carl J. Peter Lecture entitled Preaching the Word of God. Pictured with the Archbishop are Fr. James Quigley, O.P., holder of the Carl J. Peter Chair of Homiletics (left), Fr. Val Peter (brother of Fr. Carl Peter), and Msgr. James Checchio. During the lecture Archbishop Wuerl offered the following words to the alumni and students of the College: *"As a good shepherd the priest can neither guide in the ways of the truth — his prophetic ministry — nor heal what has been broken — his pastoral ministry — by isolating or separating these two dimensions of the same rich, Christ-like ministry. From the pulpit the priest must proclaim the truth — the complete and unvarnished truth — that is the way to salvation. As confessor, counselor and spiritual guide, the priest meets the members of his flock where they are to support and walk with them on their pilgrimage to the Father. Uniting clarity and compassion, as Jesus did, is an essential component of preaching the Word of God in every generation, but more than ever in our own time when so many have drifted so far from God."*

RIGHT: The Rector, Msgr. Checchio, with alumni outside the Villa Santa Caterina.

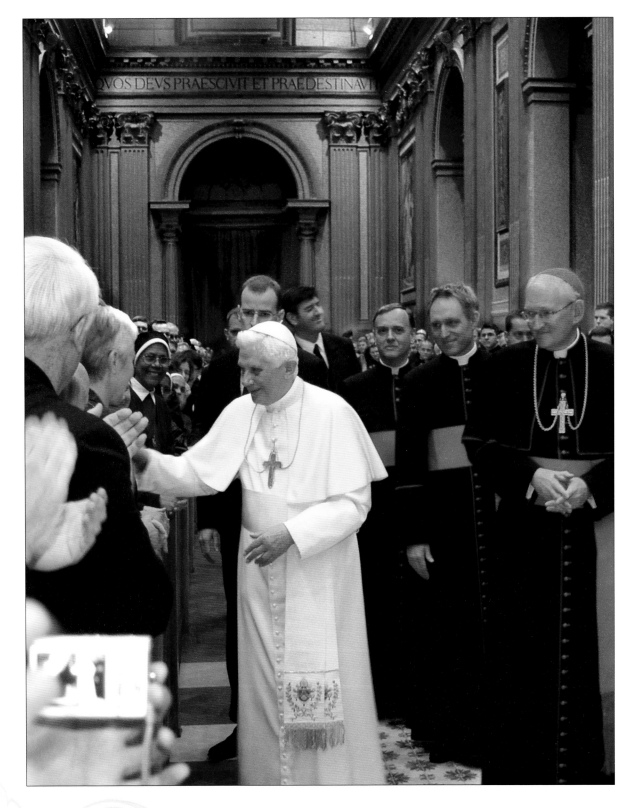

LEFT AND ABOVE: In a private audience on January 9, 2010, the Holy Father, Pope Benedict XVI, individually greeted every member of the College community, including alumni present for the anniversary celebrations.

ABOVE: Pope Benedict XVI delivers his address to the College community, during which he spoke to the institution's unique ability to help the Church of the United States cultivate a genuinely Catholic culture and bring the vision of the faith to influence issues currently facing American society.

LEFT: The Holy Father gathers with the bishops in attendance at the private audience.

PAGE 172: The Class of 2009 following the Diaconate Ordination in St. Peter's Basilica.

Benefactors

We are grateful to the following benefactors who have so generously contributed to the Finch Memorial Fund established in memory of a much beloved and proud alumnus, Rev. G. William Finch '88 of the Archdiocese of Washington. The North American College also gratefully acknowledges the generous contributions of alumni and friends to the December 8th Annual Appeal in honor of the College's 150th anniversary. Contributions to the Finch Memorial Fund and the December 8th Annual Appeal have greatly assisted us in underwriting the College's Sesquicentennial celebrations, including this anniversary book.

Archdiocese of Washington

St. John Neumann Catholic Church Parish

St. Peter's on Capitol Hill Catholic Church

Dr. Nicholas and Mrs. Joyce Babiak

Mr. Lawrence and Mrs. Mary Boesch

Rev. William D. Byrne '93

Mr. Donald and Mrs. Mabel Champagne

Rev. Msgr. James F. Checchio '92, C'97

Rev. Rory T. Conley '89

Rev. James E. Connell '87

Mr. Joseph and Mrs. Evelyn Cunningham

Rev. Roger F. DiBuo '89

Rev. Kevin G. Donovan '87

Rev. Msgr. Thomas M. Duffy '54

Rev. John N. Fell '88, C'02

Mr. and Mrs. Christopher Frechette

Rev. Msgr. Gregory W. Gordon '87

Rev. Carter H. Griffin '04

Rev. Steven O'Hala '88, C'95

Most Rev. Bernard Hebda '89

Rev. William Hegedusich

Rev. Msgr. Ronny E. Jenkins '89

Rev. William T. Kelly '88, C'95

Rev. Mark D. Knestout '97

Mrs. Lorraine La Valley

Mr. Dennis and Mrs. Pamela Lucey

Mr. James P. Lucier, Jr.

Rev. Daniel J. Mahan '88

Rev. Mark S. Mallak '88

Dr. and Mrs. Lorenzo Marcolin

Mr. Timothy J. May

His Eminence Theodore E. Cardinal McCarrick

Rev. D. Stephen McCrate '89

Rev. Msgr. Daniel Mueggenborg '89

Rev. Michael J. Murray '76

Rev. Adam Y. Park '05

Rev. Msgr. Joseph A. Ranieri '58, ICTE F'98

Rev. Patrick J. Riffle, Jr. '08

Rev. Vincent Rigdon ICTE F'06

Rev. Brian P. Sanderfoot '04

Rev. Msgr. K. Bartholomew Smith '97

Rev. Msgr. Peter J. Vaghi '85, C'88

The Honorable George B. Walsh

Rev. Dean Wilhelm '88

Most Rev. Donald W. Wuerl '67

Mr. Gary E. Young

Ms. Bernadette Zaker

Ms. Suzanne Ziemer

Acknowledgements

This book in commemoration of the 150th Anniversary of the Pontifical North American College is the result of much dedication and hard work. The College would like to thank all those who have helped see this project to completion.

To the faculty, staff, and students who labored intensely on the project, in particular:

Rev. Msgr. Daniel Mueggenborg, Rev. Dennis Yurochko, Rev. John Costello, Mrs. Mary Di Donato, Mrs. Elena Panti, Rev. Daniel Champoli, Rev. Mr. Llane Briese, Mr. Philip Smith, Mr. Gregory Jewell, Ms. Laura Panarese, Mrs. Meredith Berry, Mr. Michael Severance, Rev. Robert Young, Rev. James DeViese

To the student photographers:

Rev. Ernest Cibelli, Rev. Seamus Griesbach, Rev. Mr. Daniel O'Mullane, Mr. Mark Payton, Mr. Brian Soliven, Mr. Matthew Grady, Mr. Carmelo Morales

To those who helped with scanning and editing:

Mr. Joseph W. McQuaide IV, Mr. Jay Bananal, Mr. James Mangan

To those who helped with the book creation and production:

G. Scott Mindrum, Chad Wehrle, Maria Sheeran, Jonathan A. Schaffner, Deloris Swaisgood, Kate Johantgen, and Todd Severtson of Making Everlasting Memories; Brian Frank, Rebecca Adkins Ashcraft, Nina McCoy, and BJ Roberts of PrintManagement

To Service Corporation International for its generous contributions in underwriting this project.

Historical information has been taken from the following sources:

McNamara, Robert. *The American College in Rome.* Rochester: The Christopher Press, 1956.

Seminarians of the North American Pontifical College. *Roman Echoes: College Centennial 1859-1959.* Vatican City: Vatican Press, 1959.

North American Pontifical College. *Roman Echoes of the North American College: An Historical Collection From the Life and Experiences of its Recent Years.* 1975.

"I have looked into your eyes with my eyes.
I have put my heart near your heart."

- Pope John XXIII